The women of the Mayflower and women of Plymouth colony

J. R. C. Noyes

D0880211

Alpha Editions

This edition published in 2019

ISBN : 9789353703615

Design and Setting By
Alpha Editions
email - alphaedis@gmail.com

The Women of the Mayflower

and

Women of Plymouth Colony

By

Ethel J. R. C. Noyes

Plymouth, Massachusetts
1921

Linotyped and Printed by Memorial Press, Plymouth, Mass.

FOREWORD.

The Pilgrim Women have been written about so little that it is indeed a pleasure to welcome a book bearing the title, "The Women of the Mayflower and Plymouth Colony." History has dwelt long and minutely upon the Pilgrim Fathers and their great adventure, but has passed over the women with a generalization and occasionally a tribute. Even their contemporaries have had but little to say about them. The author of this little book is to be highly commended therefore for this much needed addition to our meagre store of literature about the mothers of this Nation.

There is much need to-day to perpetuate their spirit, to practise their faith, to maintain their ideals. They loved liberty and endured hardship, sacrifice and suffering for its sake. They built the homes of the Nation on the foundation of English ideals of home and family life which we cherish to-day as ours. They served their homes and the community life of the colony with loyal and unswerving devotion. They brought up their families in those rugged virtues and a living faith in God,

without which nations perish. They have a message for us to-day, calling us back, not to their austerities but to their righteousness and spirituality. Such books as this help to spread that message throughout the Nation.

(Signed) ANNE ROGERS MINOR,

President General,

National Society, Daughters of the American
Revolution.

The Women of the Mayflower

and

Women of Plymouth Colony

Contents

THE GREAT NORTH ROAD.

Part of design of sampler made by Lora Standish. May be
seen in Pilgrim Hall, Plymouth.

THE GREAT NORTH ROAD.

THREE HUNDRED and a few more years ago the Great North Road leading from London to Edinburgh ran through and by an English village in Nottinghamshire just as it had done three hundred years earlier than that and as it has these three hundred years. The streets of the village ran toward it and into it as brooks flow to a river, it being the main thoroughfare of travel and therefore source of all outside interests for the inhabitants of the village.

At the corner as one could say, of one of these little streets or roads where it joined the Great Road, one spring day of the sixteenth century, we might see a group of some of the villagers, young people principally, and it is plain some event of unusual interest has called them together; they are laughing and waving to a young man who rides away from them down the road, a friend who has been one of them from childhood and popular as evidenced by the number who have been wishing him a safe journey and all the usual farewells of any time and place. This young man with the pleasing face and manner is the son of the postmaster of the village and he goes to college; his erstwhile companions gaze after his retreating figure down the Great Road through the meadows and

farm lands and there is one girl looks the longest —
a girl named Mary.

Other times other manners in some things — yet
even today in another country village we have seen
the postmaster's son leave home for college, not on
horseback but in an automobile, and a gay crowd of
his friends seeing him off, his presence to be missed
in much the same degree as among those we are now
viewing with the mind's eye. Though time and
circumstance be the result of the passing of three
hundred years, human nature remains as unchanged
as the sky and sea; the student of the present whom
we mention may be cousin of a Cabinet official, that
scarcely is remembered at the moment, neither is it
thought of that the boy who rides on the Great
Northern Road is a member of one of the most sub-
stantial county families, with powerful friends
ecclesiastical and lay. As the turn of the road will
soon take him from sight, he looks back at the group
watching him for a final wave of his hat, then rides
on towards his destination, Cambridge, thinking,
perhaps, of the gentle Mary, whom we have noted,
whose fine character and winning ways are already
an influence with him and not thinking at all, or
knowing, of another Mary who is to be perhaps an
equal if not more potent influence in his life — a
woman in as great a contrast in rank and circumstance as the difference may be between a queen and
a village maid.

The gay group now lessens as some turn their
steps towards their daily tasks, a few of the boys

perchance to a long walk to the nearest school, few
and far between in those days; others to help in
the farm work, if parents could not spare them;
the girls to look after the flocks on the Commons, or
home work, such as cooking, wool spinning, caring
for the children or the sick. In this time and locality no hospitals, orphanages or homes for the aged
were there to relieve the sick or homeless; friendship and charity must indeed have reached a crest
among these only moderately well to do people,
education was backward from conditions easily
found, yet a thread of knowledge of life in other
countries as well as their own came almost daily to
these quiet, rustic people, not by books or news-
papers, (the first seen rarely, the last not existing),
nor by letters which were not publicly delivered by
the government until some time later, but by the
constant travellers on foot or on horseback by the
Great Road. The post house, both an inn, relay
station and receptible for news, though not a post
office as is today thought of by the words, was the
finest house in this particular town and well known,
from the north country to London. The position
of postmaster was a coveted benefaction of the government, the salary being large and enabling the
official to lease the manor house from a wealthy
ecclesiastic. The office at this time had been retained in one family for several generations. Thus
the men and women and children, of course, had
plenty to talk about beside their local interests at
gatherings at the inn or after church services on

Sundays, for the old Church still was revered and
followed, the changes that were coming to some of
its then supporters not yet discernable.

As we have selected a spring day for our glimpse
into this long ago life we may hear conversation
among our young friends of the coming May Day
fetes and procession of mummers and maskers, and
plans being formed and opinions given as to who
should act the usual characters in the masque of
Robin Hood. It was a pity indeed that "Will"
would not be with them this year; who might be
Alan a Dale in his stead? But Will was graver
since learning Latin and Greek, perhaps he would
not care for their good times as much as he used to.
A mistake surely — Will was just as sociable and
genial as ever.

Thus Mary and an Alice and Elizabeth and
another Mary and Katherine chatted away of coming pleasures and absent friends as blithe as any
similar bevy of girls in a far futured century from
theirs can do.

In front of one of the cottages another group has
gathered; a peddler has come in and the older
women have let the brew and baking wait a few
moments to hear the news of the towns he has come
from on his chain of travel, where other friends
dwell, and to see his merchandise. The girls' eyes
gleam as they join the listeners and prospective buy-
ers, departing Will and coming dances forgotten
for the moment in this new interest of the day.
Joy! Patty, across the river, has sent a message to

Bess; not a written note, oh, no, for neither she
could write nor Bess could read it, but a message
well delivered by the friendly vender of trifles, so
why give a thought to a lack of ability to read or
write just then, when one has learned, nevertheless,
the latest important event in the life of a dear friend
in her very own words. The peddler was a reliable
and patient transmitter of words or gifts; a tele-
phone and parcel post in one, and always a welcome
visitor. Today he might be telling of the pageant
lately given in a city not far away in distance, but
far in fact to them, to entertain the Queen on a visit
she had made there in the interests of the enterprise
and industry that "Good Queen Bess" endeavored
to prosper in her land. Fashions were also described,
as the old time peddlers were indeed specialists in
much beside selling commodities and fancies. It is
decided that Molly "shall have a new ribbon to tie
in her nut brown hair." A new clasp knife is
needed by some one;—listen to the tale of the
strange vegetables now being brought for the nobles
and gentry from the place called the Queen's kitchen
garden in Holland. He had seen them and they
were good to taste;—a measure of linen? yes; starch
just imported and the use explained; a looking-
glass, none too many on hand for comfort; a Bible
printed in English by a Dutch printer — he has just
sold one to the rector in a neighboring town — and
so the peddler passes by.

An arrival at the inn, later in the day, of a high
dignitary of the Church with his train of employees

made bustle about the village while horses were
changed. Towards evening, many of the people
gathered about the manor house, old in their day,
and while the sunset gleamed in the fish ponds on
the estate and touched the church's spire, they
talked of that day's and other day's events, dis-
cussed the curtailment of the commons, as the land-
lords enclosed more and more, whereof one had said
not that geese were stolen from the common but
the common taken from under the geese; stories
heard from travellers, or doubted what they could
not believe. A noted personage had passed that way
quite recently who had made more than ordinary
impression, a gentleman of the court going on an
important mission to Scotland, then quite as foreign
seeming a country as Holland, where this gentleman
had lived also. He had talked especially with Will,
the postmaster's son and seemed glad to hear about
his studies, and was altogether friendly. But few
travellers changed the course of the lives of any of
the dwellers in this community as this same pleasant
gentleman was to do for some. Could Mary have
dreamed that she should see her Will one day riding
away again, not to studies of Latin and Greek but
in company with this same gallant gentleman, to
the study and knowledge of a new world and
language, as private secretary of Queen Elizabeth's
ambassador to Holland?

Neighborly visits, while the twilight lingers after
babies are in their cradles, for recounting impressions and retelling news; thus the women of that

little village close a day like many another of which
their lives were made.
"Weaving through all the poor details
And homespun warp of circumstance
A golden woof-thread of romance."

Time to measure of several years, is spent almost
unnoted by these quiet dwellers in the village of
Scrooby, the village we have pictured; life for them
does not greatly change, but for William Brewster,
the postmaster's son, change, variety, experience,
have filled each day since Mr. Davidson, the Queen's
ambassador and advisor, called him to become his
secretary and confidential friend. The experiences
of this period both abroad and in his own country
have been narrated by many and may be read in
various writings. At the close of these interesting
years, when all things pointed to a continuance of
the brilliant life stretching before him as courtier
or politician, suddenly all was changed. One day,
news came to Scrooby, as to the rest of the country,
that Mary the Beautiful, exiled Queen of Scots, was
dead. How this event directly affected William
Brewster and brought him to his home again may
also be read elsewhere. He became once more a
country resident, welcomed and beloved by all his
old friends. The day of days dawned for Mary and
smiled upon her marriage with Will. He received
the appointment to the Scrooby post, in succession
to his father, so the old manor house became home
to Mary for many years, and as the wife of the most

respected and admired man of the community — the leader in thought and opinion, her days must have been filled with honest pride and pleasure and love for her husband and children. That these happy years should close with anxiety, distress, poverty as her portion was because of the very importance of her husband's position.

The causes which made for the startling contrast were slow in gathering yet when accumulated, the effects followed with rapidity. Naturally, as William Brewster settled back into his old place at the home of his boyhood, the differences he had noted between life on the Continent and in his native country made an ever recurrent impression. The word pictures he drew of vastly different scenes and manners, customs and dress found an ever ready audience and were recounted in the effort to broaden and educate his hearers. At the same time, he resumed acquaintance with college friends in other places and persuaded some to move into his locality.

During these years, the farmers found living much more difficult, owing to landlord's selfishness who were growing richer while their tenants grew poorer, also these country people found their religious life growing more difficult. Church and State were one, and ordered its subjects' lives from the beginning to the end; persons who did not care to be so controlled were soon made to see the error of their ways. Nevertheless, as the Bible was made accessible to more of the people from being printed in their own language, and as workers from the Con-

tinent, chiefly Holland, came to live and mix with
the English, other ideas and views were taken by
some, quite different from the long dominant ones
of the State Church.

Enough of these persons who thought alike separated from the old Church to call themselves a new
Church and held religious services among themselves
at their own houses. William Brewster was the
leader in his part of the country, and so many gladly
followed his teachings and example that the Church
tried in every way to restrain them. Brewster's
personal charm and influence, his intellect and gen-
erous spirit drew countless numbers of men and
women for miles around to his home for the worship
they conducted according to their ideas of right and
liberty of conscience. After the service in the old
Chapel of the manor house, he entertained all the
company at dinner.

Just here we can see Mary Brewster, the sympathetic and charming hostess, her fair face silhouetted
against the dark, age old wainscot of the refectory
or dining-room, of the manor inn, surrounded by her
and her husband's early friends and those of later
years, loved by them all for herself no less than as
the wife of their revered leader.

These gatherings came to be held in secret, of
necessity, as the members were liable to arrest for
absenting themselves from the regular Church services and teaching other views. Spies were set to
report their actions, and some were called before
the magistrates and sent to prison. It became plain

that they could not continue in that manner — uncertainty and anxiety becoming daily companions.

Queen Elizabeth died; her successor rode down from Scotland on the Great North Road and stopped with all his retinue at Scrooby. This was doubtless the last brilliant assembly that the manor saw, when the home of the Brewster's. The people hoped for better things at his accession, but soon learned that he was to be just as hard upon them and times would be worse. Plans were made among them under the guidance of Brewster for emigration to Holland where, as he knew, there was liberty and welcome for all.

It is not difficult to realize the reluctance with which they came to this decision, to leave all their natural associations, to give up much that was dear with almost no hope of a return. Sad indeed were these days for Mary Brewster and the other women of the community who were preparing like her to part with much of their belongings, their homes and friends who could not think as they did but were cherished, notwithstanding.

"Well worthy to be magnified are they
Who with sad hearts of friends and country took
A last farewell, their loved abodes forsook,
And hallowed ground in which their fathers lay."

The final summer for them in the old home passed; that each sunset brought a certain regret, each rose that bloomed a more than passing attention we may believe. Yet it seemed the best thing they could do for themselves and their children. In the place where they would make their new home others of English birth and similar experiences were already settled, having been, as they, forced to leave their own land; at least they would be welcomed by and could have intercourse and sympathy with those of their own race and country, advice and help also in the matter of the problem of living — a somewhat staring one, as they were ignorant of any solution but their own. Curiosity, too, supposed ever to be an attribute of women, might pierce their melancholy a little, and they had heard enough to wish to behold for themselves since the opportunity had come; the enthusiasm for adventure on the part of the children must have lightened the prospect as well. The pain was in giving up the dear interests, the fond associations of their lives.

Dull indeed the eye of fancy which cannot see Mary Brewster with her two little daughters coming down the stone steps of the manor house in a golden evening, to follow the path through the meadow fields towards Ryton stream and there wander on its banks, visiting favorite nooks and listening to the bird's good night, for them seeming notes of farewell. As Experience wears ever the same dress, her mirror must reflect for each of us some such scene as this.

THE SWORD OF THE SPIRIT.

Design of carving on pew back from old Church at Scrooby,
England.   May be seen in Pilgrim Hall, Plymouth.

THE SWORD OF THE SPIRIT.

A SHIP had been engaged to meet them at Boston from where these travellers were to sail. The first stage of their journey was accomplished by their arrival at that town. Since the edict that whoever did not subscribe to and uphold the State Church must leave the country, one would suppose that their proposed departure would not have been difficult, but when it was discovered how many desired to go and had so arranged, malice itself must have been the cause of the refusal of the authorities to permit it. The ship's master then had to be well paid to consent to take them away in secret. Instead of meeting them at the appointed time in daylight, he kept them waiting until night, but they all were finally on board with their baggage. Before the ship had gotten a fair start, however, they were stopped by the port authorities who had been warned by the ship's owner, himself. The voyagers were taken from the ship back to the town in small boats, their belongings examined and those of most value as well as all their money taken from them, the women having to undergo as thorough a search of their persons as the men, which their own chronicler speaks of with indignation. Still further embarrassment awaited these women when they were all marched through the town in the early morning and

people hurried into the streets to stare at them as
at a spectacle, and followed them into the court
room. Here the magistrates were more favorably
disposed toward them but were obliged to order
their imprisonment until the Lords in Council
should decide their case. After a month's confine-
ment, which was made only less trying and uncomfortable by the kind hearted magistrates — to their
great credit—the women and children and most of
the men were dismissed and sent back whence they
came, by order of the Council; the more prominent
men were kept till the autumn was far advanced
before their freedom was granted.

The wounds to their feelings were healed by determination, and after an unexpected winter among
their friends, who in vain urged the abandonment of
their plans, some of them were ready to make a
second attempt to accomplish their object.

Brewster and several men, especially his friend,
John Robinson, made other and as they thought
safer arrangements for this venture. So one bleak
day at the end of the winter, the women and children, with the necessary baggage, embarked in a
small boat at an inconspicuous place on the coast,
and sailed out on the sea. The large boat chartered
for the voyage was to await them at an appointed
place near the shore, between Grimsby and Hull,
and the men were to go by land to meet it and
the small boat bringing their families and possessions; all were to board it, and hoping for a
more trusty master of this ship before news of their

plans would get to unfriendly ears, would be away.
Such good time was made by the little boat from
shore to rendezvous, that it reached the appointed
place before the larger ship arrived and must ride
at anchor in a choppy sea. The women being unac-
customed to travel by sea were most uncomfortable,
and the weather becoming worse, with the boat
pitching and tossing so continuously they were
driven to desperation and begged the seamen to run
the boat into an inlet where the water was quiet,
that they might have some rest. The men evidently
compassionate, did so, but it was a most unfortunate
move, though seemingly harmless. The night was
spent in that strange and lonely place, while their
thoughts must have been busy with questionings as
to the non-arrival of the ship and the possibility of
the men being arrested before they could get to
them; the cold was penetrating and in their efforts
to keep the children warm and quiet, the keeping up
of their own courage was under long odds.

In the dimness of the dawn, they could see the
ship making anchor, and on shore, their men could
also be seen, so hope arose with the morning, soon
to be overcast, however, when it was realized that
their little boat was fast on shore, and no chance
of release till the tide rose. The resourceful Dutch
captain of the larger ship, endeavoring to honestly
earn his money, sent his own small boat to shore to
gain time by taking on the men. These activities
gave the children some entertainment at least, we
suppose, and they doubtless waved and called to

their fathers and friends as the first boat load left
shore and boarded the ship; the second trip was
begun when suddenly the watchful captain saw an
armed company appearing in the distance; one
glance and his efforts were all in the direction of
getting himself and his boat to safety, no matter
who might be on it or who not on it. His sails were
quickly run up, his anchor raised, notwithstanding
the entreaties of the men, who also realized the situation, to send them ashore, at least, if he would not
stay. The plight of the women and children, help-
less onlookers of this tragic end of their plans, drove
the men wellnigh frantic, both on the ship and on
shore. The ship was soon out of sight, flying before
a good wind, but into as great a storm as they left
breaking behind.

Quick consultation among the remaining men decided who should try to escape and who would
remain with the women. It was wiser that not all
should be taken this time if it could be avoided.
Some of them, therefore, thus leaving their friends
and families in this dire situation, got safely away,
though their position was no more enviable than
those husbands and brothers who were taken away
on the ship. No marvel that the women, even the
bravest, were heartsick and in tears, with their
husbands apparently lost and the children, frightened, cold and sobbing, clinging to them. But
they had two or three of the men, and well could
Mary Brewster be a tower of strength to most,
seeing her own husband still on the shore and know-

ing what a rock he would be for them all to lean on.

When the company of men on horseback and on foot came to the water's edge, where the boatload of women and the few men awaited their fate at their hands, they placed them under arrest and hurried them to the nearest town, to the court.

With their former experience in mind, they anticipated a long, dreary imprisonment; but unlooked for circumstances pleaded their cause. Each magistrate before whom they were taken in turn, with ever increasing haste, seemed anxious to shelve the responsibility of a sentence. Their case seemed so innocent and pitiable, the appearance of so many despondent women and chilled and shivering children, so appealing, that no justice could harden his heart sufficiently to imprison them, more especially when their only crime seemed to be the desire to be with their husbands, wherever they went, which was certainly a compliment to men in general. When urged to go to their homes, their reply that they had no longer any homes, capped the climax, and, fearing criticism of any harsh treatment, the magistrates were most eager to be rid of the matter on any excuse to themselves. Without realizing it, as the nerves of the women were strained to the breaking point, they certainly affected the nerves of the men, and when the judges dismissed them, finally, from sheer desperation, even the men of the company being included, it would have been hard to say which parted from the other with most pleasure.

That day's experience, in all its misery, however,

advertised them in an unimagined way, for, though
they only desired an inconspicuous and quiet life,
the story of their wanderings and hardships was
soon talked of and many came to hear of them and
consider their cause with interest and sympathy,
and, indeed, led to their making new friends and
gaining help later on. Nevertheless, their weariness
was far from over, and, throughout that spring,
Brewster and Robinson, in the face of other disap-
pointments and difficulties, used their final resources
to get the women and children and themselves out
of their net of trouble.

Yet in the end their dauntless efforts were successful. Their own historian tells us that, notwithstanding, they all got away after a time and "met
together again according to their desires, with no
small rejoicing."

This happy place of meeting and rejoicing was
Amsterdam, the city of their intentions when planning to leave England. The comparing of adven-
tures since they had been swept apart by the tumul-
tuous circumstances of their departure must indeed
have been a refreshment to their minds as the safe
arrival at their destination gave rest to their bodies.

The anticipated welcome of the English people,
who had already settled in the city and had churches
for worship according to their several ideals, was
cordial and sympathetic. We may be sure that the
women of the longer residence were only too happy

to show and tell of this wonderful city, to the newcomers, and that the women in whom we are especially interested would have been glad indeed that
such guides and advisors should have been there to
help them assimilate the countless new impressions
which were next in the path of their experience.
While each old friend or comparatively new
acquaintance who had been of their original party
at home, must have grown doubly dear by similar
situation in the surrounding strangeness of this new
world with all its marvels and perplexities. The
contrast between the quiet existence they had led so
long and the bustling, colorful life into which they
were plunged, might well have dazed them for a
time had not a certain sort of commotion and
change attended them, in the interval, and been an
unforseen preparation for steadiness in any confusion of circumstance.

We may picture Mary Brewster, an example of
their steadfast purpose, meeting the new and trying
conditions of poverty, a new language and different
modes of living in calm cheerfulness. Love and loyalty to the men of their families would actuate every
woman to do her best in making the homes these same
men had now to struggle to provide. Mutual understanding and common interests were great factors
in smoothing the rough places. These men, now or
afterwards, never thought of going first as pioneers
to provide a home for their wives and sisters to
come to; they well knew that the women were the
ones to make the homes for them. It was such a

matter of course that the question seems never to
have arisen, likewise never commented on; one of
the reasons why we encounter such a scarcity of
details that we would gladly read in their records.

At this time even the names of the women seem
hidden as by the very secrecy of their journeyings.
Later the mist clears for us somewhat. Only the
figures of Mary Brewster and her young daughters,
Fear and Patience, Mrs. Robinson, the pastor's wife,
and her daughters are comparatively clearly out-
lined in the picture we try to see just here.

Nevertheless, it was because of a woman and her
clothes, especially a velvet hood, that was a prime
cause of their moving from this scarcely established
home; even as the long shadow of a woman had already fallen indirectly upon them in their original
home and ultimately made for their departure
thence.

Let us seem to be standing on the banks of a canal
of Amsterdam. It is a brilliant winter afternoon
and the scene is animated and full of color, for skaters are flying over the ice and spectators are watching them or walking about. Here is a group of
women, there are one or two whom we recognize,
at least, having seen them in England. The wife
of the pastor of the Separatist Church which is
seeking a home, Mrs. Robinson, and the wife of the
leader of his congregation, Mrs. Brewster, with them
a lady much more elaborately dressed than either of
them, the wife of the pastor of the Separatist Church
already established in Amsterdam, Mrs. Johnson. We

feel quite sure it is she, for what is the advantage of having fine clothes if one may not wear them where many can see, on a gay afternoon in a big city especially, and has it not been a matter of indifference to her what comments are made or how nearly her husband's church is rent asunder? These new friends are a pleasure to her since they do not criticize but only admire her appearance. Their attitude, if reflected from the male members of their party is that the style of woman's costume is a detail, and may be according to her station, the one point being that it should be paid for.

Mrs. Johnson is probably giving her point of view of the matter and an opinion of her brother-in-law, in the controversy, which is a matter of record. Meanwhile, the eyes of the mothers see the bright faces of their children, and their voices come to them from the ice. John and Jonathan are being called to by a number of girls as they start to race to a goal.

The girls have some of their new friends with them, fair English roses like themselves, all for the present blooming together in this country of tulips — Bridget and Mercy Robinson, Fear and Patience Brewster, Jacquelin and Dorothy May, the latter, daughters of the elder of Mr. Johnson's church. Dorothy and Patience, lighthearted children, never giving thought to the web Fate is weaving for them. Soon to part, after a brief acquaintance, but to renew it in a few years, because Dorothy is a magnet to draw back to Amsterdam the grave young

man so frequently seen with her father and Mr.
Brewster, at this time, and will herself leave her
home there to join these friends again. And
Patience is to become the wife of a man of prominence and influence just as her mother had done.
These are future visions indeed, yet these two girls,
as they stand side by side, are the presentment of
the women (though ship and Colony were then un-
dreamed of) causing the special designation in the
title of this story.

Therefore because of the turmoil regarding Mrs.
Johnson's apparel and other matters affecting the
congregation, John Robinson and William Brewster
thought it wiser to remove their people from such
ensuing contentions, notwithstanding it would entail
the search for new employments and cause some
more expense.

It was ever the Sword of the Spirit — the spirit
of self-sacrifice, "whatsoever it should cost them,"
to attain their cherished object, democratic religious
and civil government, that led them onward, step
by step, to the victory which was to be theirs.

This change of surroundings was accomplished
with much less stress and strain than their former
one. Their new companions in Amsterdam were
sorry to have them go; while a welcome from strangers awaited them in the city of their choice.

UNDER THE LINDENS OF LEYDEN.

UNDER THE LINDENS OF LEYDEN.

THE CHIMES from the spire of the State House rang out an evening hour. There seemed no unusual portent in this daily custom to the ear of workers in the busy city turning homewards at close of day. Yet in that hour on that calm evening of early summer, history was being made for that city, and to its honored name was added an interest for thousands of a future day by the seemingly unimportant event then taking place.

A large canal boat, one of the many that plied between Amsterdam and Leyden, was nearing its mooring at the close of the day's trip and a number of persons were on the quay apparently awaiting its arrival. The boat was heavily ladened with freight and passengers, the household belongings and persons of a number of families. If some of the members looked a trifle anxious, all seemed happy and still interested in all to be viewed at the end of a pleasant journey that had been full of new sights for the majority. A pleasanter voyage than many had experienced within the year, and with much uncertainty and strangeness eliminated from this landing at Leyden which had harassed their arrival at Amsterdam; for these are the pilgrims from England, to whom the authorities of this city had recently given permission for residence, in reply to

a petition sent in their behalf from Amsterdam, by
their pastor, John Robinson.

The English were already well known in Leyden
and some of this party had been there to rent houses
and survey the prospect. More than casual glances
were given these new arrivals, for, though evidently
poor people and certainly, as yet, unknown, their
appearance was distinguished even in their plain
clothes of English fashion, different to the gay apparel of the natives.

The accounts of this beginning of their sojourn
in a new locality are somewhat meagre, nevertheless
they furnish ground for speculation and conclusions
not unjustified. Our interest follows the women we
already know and others whom we are soon to know,
as they once more endeavor to solve the problems
of home-keeping with slender resources, their characteristics of patience and courage again to the test.
An admonition surely given by their beloved pastor
must have dwelt in their thoughts to "stand fast
in one spirit, with one mind striving together . . .
and in nothing terrified."

The advantages of living in a prosperous, pro-
gressive and highly civilized city were not long in
being realized by these women. Though, at first,
their homes were in the poorer part of the city, their
industry and energy supplementing that of the men,
who soon found plenty of employment in the trades
of the city, particularly the cloth and silk weaving,
enabled them to live fairly comfortably. The mar-
kets of fish and vegetables saw them as daily

customers, and even the flower market found them as occasional visitors to delight the children as well as themselves. The public schools gave to many of the children more of an education than their mothers had had; this opportunity for free knowledge, as well as the hospitals, homes for the aged, orphan asylums, were some of the marvels of this new life. Books and pictures were so moderate in price as to be available for all.

The contrasts between the conditions which tended towards the benefit and advancement of the plain people in their present home and those which were only for the benefit of the wealthy and aristocratic class in their old home were as easily seen by his companions now as they had been by William Brewster years before.

The objects above all the planning for the routine of practical life were that they might have food and comfort, peace and quiet to worship God.

They were not without news of England, for their community was constantly increased by new arrivals, who, hearing of the success of their venture, came to try the experiment themselves; some remaining as true friends and burden sharers, others returning.

Scarcely three years passed before the women had the joy of moving into attractive newly built cottages on a piece of ground in a very desirable location for their needs, bought by several of the men for all in common. All were now in good circumstances retained by continual labor, however.

The nearness of the famous University was a satisfaction to the many intellectual men of the party,
both to enter as students or to read in its library.

That the content of the men was reflected by the
women is without doubt, for if the men in a family
are fairly happy it is easy for the women to be so,
and, on their own account they had reason to be
lighthearted. Their cosy little houses were built at
the sides of the piece of property, the center becoming a small park or community garden with sanded
walks, flower bordered. The pastor's house, at one
end, was the largest and finest, for in it the Sunday
services and three teaching services or lectures were
held, as they had been held in the old manor house
in Scrooby.

Besides their two indefatigable and honored leaders, the pastor and William Brewster, now an elder
in their Church, the community was fortunate in
having among them the young doctor, a widower,
whose home was kept by his sister, Anna. Her self-
reliant, decisive character must have been highly
sympathetic and congenial to her brother. The life
of Anna Fuller is one of those most discernable to
us in that coterie of women, after the lapse of the
long years. Tactful and clever she was, and a favorite with all. Between her and Mary Brewster
there grew a warm attachment.

A friend to them both and to many others, was
Katherine Carver (the wife of John Carver, a
prominent and valued man of their company) whose
lovely character endeared her to them, but whose

chief interest in life was her husband and what concerned him.

Ann Tilly and the wife of James Chilton added to
the group of these young matrons who enjoyed their
quiet but not altogether uneventful lives in mutual
sympathy and esteem. We must admire the smooth-
ness with which they managed their affairs, taking
into consideration the varying temperaments among
them; tact and unselfishness, wisdom and charitable-
ness must indeed have been taught them by "the
grave Mistress Experience," and not only among
themselves was it observable, but also with their
new, interested and friendly neighbors, the women
of that Dutch city, through whom they became ac-
quainted with its manners and customs and to feel
quite familiar with them. Their children and the
Dutch children soon became friends and through
them the mothers of each began their knowledge of
one another, to their mutual advantage. We know
the pride of the native women in their city and how
ready and willing they were to show its sights and
relate its history to these interested strangers.

Thus we can easily fancy a party coming along
Belfry Lane and through other streets on their way
to visit the Burg, a promised treat to the children
and desired by their elders. Ann Tilly is taking the
children of her household — two little cousins and a
niece — having none of her own, whom she has mothered. Mistress Chilton has with her, her daughter;
Mary Brewster and her two daughters walk with
Katherine Carver; Anna Fuller and the Carpenter

girls — one soon to be her sister-in-law — and one
or two boys, a lively party, all accompanied by some
Dutch friends as guides.

Leyden was at that time full of reminders of the
war with Spain, its part of it having been the great
siege. Up on the Burg the country for miles around
lies before them, and as they look, the story is told
and they try to picture just where and how the bat-
tle was fought. Doubtless some old soldier was on
the Burg, that bright afternoon, living for himself
again that time of suffering and valor, and glad to
recount many of the details and describe where had
been a particular Spanish redoubt, or just where
such a regiment had been stationed, or the location
of a General's headquarters.

We of days far from theirs are yet joined to their
experiences of that afternoon of our fancy if we
have chanced on a similar recital from one who had
participated in another war with Spain in a very
different country and setting, a war in which the
descendants of some of these women had a part.
From the wall of an old Spanish castle near Manila,
a party of women, one of them the present writer,
looked over the surrounding plain on an afternoon
not many years ago, while the then American owner,
their host, related just such details and anecdotes
of the Philippine incident in the war with Spain,
already some years in the past; there was a battery
of the United States regulars; the insurgents came
in here; a far glimpse of the sunlit harbor showed
where Dewey's ships lay; and so on. By such a

touch does a string on the harp of life sing on
through the centuries.

Coming home, they would visit the City Hall,
where were then kept many mementos and relics of
victory upon which they could look with wondering
earnestness, feeling as we when today viewing objects closely connected with the World War, so recently in our thoughts.

The blossoms of the lindens fell over the grey wall
enclosing the old cloister wherein the veiled nuns
had walked, fell over into another garden and
around other women of whom the cloistered nuns
had never heard, and to whom they were but a
name; lives in deepest contrast, lived in neighboring
environment yet divided by a grey stone wall and
many years.

At a well by the old wall several young women
have gathered, some to get water for their household
use, others to meet them there for a gossip — for
even in the little colony of English Separatists living so quietly on their own ground, itself almost a
cloister, in the gay city of Leyden there was, of
course, gossip in its friendly and sociable meaning.
But chat between the women only is interrupted,
and apparently to their amusement, by small boys
and girls all eagerness at a tale one of their number
is telling of an exciting event in their school life
that day; no less than the story of how the Prince's
ball fell into the canal and he took the boat hook

belonging to an old woman who lived near, never thinking she would object, and fished the ball safely out. A tale with an apparently happy ending, but not so, the old woman mistaking Prince Frederick for just an everyday boy scolded him well, and when some one called out that it was the Prince who had borrowed her boat hook, she was so overcome and frightened that she ran in her house and they could not coax her out, for she said they would take her to prison.

Smiles fade as a shadow of remembrance crosses the minds of some of the listeners at prison experiences they have known, and perhaps a thought of contrast that here, in this democratic land, their children have as playmate a prince of the blood, while in their own country they might scarcely ever have seen one. A few of the young men have wandered towards the well, since evening is advancing and their day's employments are over; here are Edward Southworth, William Bradford, Robert Cushman, William White,— and, severally, Alice Carpenter, Mary Singleton and Anna Fuller may no longer be monopolized by the children, while Patience Brewster is glad to hear of her friend in Amsterdam, Dorothy May, from William Bradford, who visits Elder May rather frequently.

In fact, news from Amsterdam was quite regularly brought by visitors as well as by those of their own company returning, since seeds of romance sown in the early days of their sojourn were bearing fruit, and engagements were so frequent that one was scarcely talked of before another came up for consideration.

Thus it was not surprising to see Samuel Fuller leaning across the half door of the Carpenter's cottage, while Agnes, presumably waiting for Alice to return from the well, on the other side of the door, smiled at him. Not unlikely that Edward South-worth and the doctor will both be asked to supper, for the Carpenter household, with five gay, pretty girls in it was not a dull one. One of the households soonest to break away, however, from the present surroundings; after three of his daughters married, Alexander Carpenter moved the rest of his family to his old home in England. Anna Fuller noticing her brother's absorption and knowing from rather frequent experience that he may forget about the supper she will provide for him, decides on spending the evening away from home, herself. To her neighbor and special friend, Mary Allerton, she will be a gladly welcomed guest — she who, a year ago was Mary Norris, and for whom Anna had been a witness at her marriage to Isaac Allerton. Sarah, Isaac's sister, who lived with them, was good company also, and if Degory Priest should happen by, as was more than likely, to walk with Sarah to the weekly lecture at Pastor Robinson's and if William White should come too, still less unlikely, she would tell him that — "yes she would marry him, when Samuel married Agnes Carpenter and was off her hands and mind."

In this group of pilgrims there were many young

men and girls, therefore many were the love tales
told under the lindens and marriages frequent
during their sojourn.

The Botanical Gardens at Leyden, one of the
city's proud possessions, must have held the usual
charm for walks of sweethearts and wives and the
men of their choice on a Sunday afternoon that
seems to be evident everywhere there are Gardens,
in any era and place, from Edinburgh to Hong
Kong.

The annual Kermiss also witnessed many visitors
from among these strangers, and the other holidays
and sports came in time to be almost as familiar and
enjoyable as though known in their own country.

Good health and fairly comfortable living made
comparatively light hearts, among the younger set
especially.

We are glad to picture these years of their life
in Leyden when their industry and thrift brought
them to pleasant days of living, and the cheerfulness
and peace of their little community attracted visitors and favorable comments. These days were
lighted by hope, a hope that they might through
some fortunate possibility be able to return to their
beloved England and live in the unmolested peace
and independence there which they had found here.

Prosperity again found Mary Brewster, for her
husband becoming a much respected teacher of
languages in the University, was soon able to win
a comfortable and adequate living for his family,
and, as always, the Brewsters were ever ready with

sympathy and help to those less well off than they; indeed one of the chief supports in this thoroughly religious body of people was their convention of mutual help and friendliness.

Mary, as well as her husband, was always available as the confidant of their neighbors, therefore a frequent witness for the young couples who went to the State House, according to the custom of the country, to declare their intentions of marriage, and we feel sure the interest did not stop there, and that she and her daughters helped with the simple festivities connected with these marriages. A member of the University was exempt from tax on homemade wines and brew, and as both were common beverages at that time, and made in all households, her wine and cooking receipts must have been frequently used.

While the history of these Pilgrims may be told, and has been, with casual if any reference to the women, the story of the women must hinge on reference to the whole Pilgrim story. Looking at them from our position, down the long vista, seeing the background of which they were hardly conscious, the foreground invisible to them, their reality and aliveness should be vividly lighted by all the colors of romance which only distance may give and we should be able to get the feeling that things had for them, at least. A few plain, loyal, trustful women living their daily lives with no dream of a place in history, yet on whom else may we look entitled to a softer, more caressing glow from the flame of fame?

Julianna Carpenter, the eldest sister, married George Morton, before the lindens bloomed again, followed soon by the marriages of Agnes to the wise and popular young doctor, the doctor's sister to William White, as she had said, and the lively young widow, Sarah, sister of Isaac Allerton, to Degory Priest. Their mutual satisfaction and happiness was punctured by the shock of the sudden death of one of their number, Agnes Fuller; the whole community was stirred by the fact that so unexpectedly, the doctor was again a widower. Thus their recurring measure of joy and sorrow, pleasure and trouble, success and endeavor.

We may well hope that, in the fullness of time, our days may be looked upon with the same searchlight of sympathy and understanding which we turn upon theirs.

Another year more wedded couples were added to the list—it was a sign of their hopefulness that marriage among them was encouraged and the remarriage of the widowed favored. Alice Carpenter married Edward Southworth and William Bradford brought his bride from Amsterdam, Dorothy May. It was in the late autumn that she came to Leyden to renew some childhood's friendships. The marriage of another friend of Alice Southworth occurred at a slightly later date when Robert Cushman married Mary Singleton. So these younger and important men of the settlement took on new responsibilities, and after a while Dr. Fuller tried a third time and found with Bridget

Lee a more permanent happiness in matrimony.

The very little girls, as the years passed, were replaced by others, while they grew into the places of maidenhood left vacant by the younger matrons. Thus Mary Chilton, Bridget Robinson, Priscilla Mullins, Patience and Fear Brewster, Desire Minter, Humility Cooper, formed a lively group in which Elizabeth Tilly and Mercy Robinson claimed membership though somewhat younger.

The famous storks of Holland were good enough to bring many rosy babies to the little homes of this English colony, so the joy and amusement of babyhood was never lacking.

Into this little world a passing traveller entered, a young man of some wealth and position in England, who having heard of the community, thought to look upon it as of transient interest, and desiring to meet William Brewster, John Robinson and others whose writings printed by their own established press were attracting attention. In truth he was more interested in the printing press than the writings, being reputed himself a printer, and as a worker in one art or trade or profession desires to see the results or products of another in that same class, Edward Winslow entered the life of the Brewsters, the Robinsons, the Allertons, the Bradfords, but most particularly into the life of Elizabeth Barker, and since it was her world it became his, too, henceforth. Almost the last romance of these peaceful years witnessed by the lindens and the old grey wall.

Soon thereafter a rift became apparent in the
harmony of existence in the garden colony and it
was Mary Brewster who heard it first. Again she
experienced the haunting anxiety on her husband's
account, which she well knew of old, and from the
same source — persecution by the royal authorities
in England and their representatives in Holland.
The cause was the printing press and the sentiments
it set forth. The hunt for the unknown though
suspected printer at that time is an entertaining
story told by various chroniclers of the history of
these people and reminds one of the somewhat
similar search for the hidden printer of our modern
times who issued the prescribed little Belgian news-
paper during the occupation of that country by the
Germans.

Suddenly in addition to this personal touch of
unrest came a focus in the national affairs of their
adopted country, which centered in Leyden, and
while of great interest to them, as such matters have
been, and are, to us, are always bound to increase
uncertainty and instability of daily concerns.

The scope of the present work is not to dwell on
the general events of history, but only as their
effects touched the lives of the women of our story.
Gradually it had come to be recognized, also, that
the younger generation among them was fast becoming more Dutch than English, as was natural
from environment. And since their object had
never been other than to remain English people and
to send the enlightening word of their religious

freedom and church's independence back to their own people, now that the advantage of their printing press was about to be denied them this advancement was at an end.

These subjects for reflection and others equally compelling brought them to a point in their destiny for which Providence in the preceding years had been preparing them by the variation of their experience, the widening of their horizons, the increasing knowledge of humanity and capacity for labor and economy which came as assets of their exile from home in a land of comparative freedom.

The women had as much opportunity for facing these questions and facts and discussing them among themselves as the men, and the possibility of giving up all that they had won for the sake of their faith and ideals loomed as evident before them as to those upon whom they not only depended but supported by their love and loyalty.

Thus prior to the all-important conference called at Pastor Robinson's house, many of them had set to withdraw their thoughts from the comparative ease and prosperity of the past ten years, and drill their minds to becoming again way-farers and makers of new homes elsewhere. Where else, indeed? Many suggestions were made before the answer was determined. When it became definitely known to the city authorities that these peaceful, industrious and altogether desirable inhabitants were thinking of severing their connection with them, they announced their regret publicly in

complimentary terms. Also an offer was made that
these would-be pioneers continue under the flag of
the Netherlands as colonists. But it was their own
flag, their own nationality for which they were about
to sacrifice much and for which they stood ready
to endure more in the future.

At the assembly at John Robinson's house where
the congregation met for final decision, it was resolved that if the vote showed a majority in favor
of remaining a while longer, the Pastor should
remain with them, and for those who wished to
emigrate immediately, William Brewster, their
Elder, should be their spiritual leader, while awaiting the coming of the rest.

In regard to this vote, one writer has said, "It
cannot be known whether or not the women of the
church had a vote in the matter. Presumably they
did not, for the primitive church gave good heed
to the words of Paul, 'Let your women keep silence
in the churches.' Neither can it be known — if
they had a voice — whether the wives and daughters of some of the embarking Pilgrims, who did not
go themselves at this time, voted with their husbands
and fathers for removal." If this exactness is lacking, we may feel a certain knowledge that each
woman was aware of how the vote which affected
her and hers would be cast. One is somehow reminded of the old story, though of modern times,
of a certain pastor receiving a call to a larger field
of usefulness who retired to seek Divine guidance.
During this time a member of the congregation

called for information on the subject. The pastor's
little daughter received the visitor, and in reply to
the important question said, "I can't say exactly —
Father is praying but Mother is packing."

During the time between the actual decision and
final satisfactory arrangements for departure — we
can fancy the women's days being particularly
trying. Breaking up homes — deciding what would
be needed most in the unknown land and in the
restricted space alloted to each one's belongings
on a small ship. Cooking and table utensils were
commonly of pewter and wood — so anxiety of
modern movings regarding breakage was lessened —
books, clothing and furniture required the same
attention as we experience in packing. And looking-
glasses! Mrs. Robinson's sister, Jane White, had
married soon after their arrival in Leyden, Ran-
dolph Tickens, a manufacturer of looking-glasses,
so although the Tickens family were not to go among
the first, a looking-glass or two were certainly to be
found space for. If they were such as the mirror
of Mary, Queen of Scots, though of earlier make,
and shown to visitors in Holyrood Castle, they were
not very desirable or useful, giving but a hazy
reflection of any one's good looks — but they may
have been satisfactory when new.

The day before the breaking up of the community
came at last, as all days do, though seemingly far
off when first recognized as approaching. That
evening was spent by all, at the Pastor's house, at
supper and with music. If verging on tragedy to

us, as on-lookers, what must it have been for them?

The barges are moored at the quay — near the Nuns Bridge — were any of their thoughts flung back, as ours are, to the day of their arrival at Leyden eleven years before? This party is large, as many who would return, for a time, are going with the others to see them depart. Some have already gone and are in England making final arrangements — so Mary Brewster, Katherine Carver, and Mary Cushman are without their husbands at present — though the sons of the Brewster and Cushman families are at their mother's side — while Katherine Carver has the unfailing attention of the tall, strong, young man, devoted to her husband's interests, John Howland.

Anna Fuller White (since her marriage called more often by her full name, Susanna), has her husband and little son, Resolved, a fitting name for the first born of this woman. Her brother, the doctor, is of the emigrating party, (with a young assistant), but his wife and baby will stay behind. The children of some are to go with them, while those of others will remain with relatives — thus the little son of Dorothy and William Bradford has gone to his grand-parents at his mother's old home in Amsterdam. The sadness in the eyes of some of the women as they look back at the fair and beautiful city, which has sheltered them so kindly, is formed of regret that all may not remain together in this departure, as well as a sigh for the happy years now gone.

THE FIRE OF FAITH.

The cradle that was brought across the
sea for the first New England baby.
May be seen in Pilgrim Hall, Plymouth.

THE FIRE OF FAITH.

As ONE GOES along the road of remembrance, some readers as well as the writer may see before them the outlines of a ship at the wharf of, perhaps, an unfamiliar city, towards which they have travelled after careful planning and arrangements for a voyage which is, after all, to carry them towards the unknown —. Just so, and with the same feelings the eyes of the women passengers on the canal boats from Leyden, looked upon the form of the "Speedwell", the little ship on which their thoughts and plans had for some time focused, now appearing before them with all the suddenness of reality and accomplished effort. Those whose former knowledge of ships had been far from pleasant, saw it with bravely stiffened reluctance or repugnance, while the younger were in contrast as eager to experience this new thing.

Some of the girls, whose memories, real or imagined, could stretch back to their coming from England, almost as babies, were in great favor and admiration with those whose life and experience had been only in Holland. So Bartholomew Allerton and his little sisters, Resolved White, John Cooke, Samuel Fuller (nephew and namesake of the doctor), relied on the good nature that would reply to their numerous questionings of Humility Cooper, Desire

Minter, Mary Chilton, Elizabeth Tilly and Priscilla
Mullins, for the older boys were too interested and
too busy in the matters of moving the baggage and
the preparations on the ship to give attention to
those who had no higher travelling lineage than a
canal boat.

It was evening when they arrived at Delfshaven
and their ship could not sail until morning. That
July night was too full of excitement and emotion
for ordinary rest, even for many of the inhabitants
of the town, who were drawn to the wharves by
curiosity and interest to see this decidedly unusual
party who were to sail from their port.

Though their old tower had seen the sailing of
many a ship and the farewells of countless friends
in its centuries of guardianship of the little city, no
scene had ever been quite like this, and curiosity
turned quickly to sympathy.

Friends came also from Amsterdam to see them
sail, so that an animated picture filled the evening
and morning hours. The fatigue of the women was
forgotten or disguised in the sad enjoyment of these
last hours with the members of their families who
were not to go with them.

Fear and Patience Brewster see naught else but
their mother's face, filled with its well-known love,
sympathy and energy, as she made one more effort
at self-sacrifice and endurance for her husband's
sake, choosing to go with him and two of her boys
who would need her more in the new life than the
two daughters, left to the protection of their oldest

brother and the care of the Robinsons and other
loyal friends in the safety and comfort of their
Leyden home, cheering them and others with the
prospects of a speedy reunion. Hope and courage
gilded these prospects at the time. Sarah Priest,
who is to have the care of little Sarah Allerton, her
namesake niece, has her husband to part from, as
well as her brother and his gentle wife. The doctor's
wife has a similar farewell to make to her husband,
though her sister-in-law goes with her family —
husband and son — and the wife of Edward Fuller
goes with him and their son. Susanna White having
all with her whom she holds most dear (her brothers,
her husband and little boy) may be looked upon as
one of the most fortunate of the company; it is the
friends of Anna Fuller (as she still seems to them)
who remain behind, who shall have heavier thoughts
at parting than Susanna White, though her cheerfulness and kindness are not wanting.

Other women who are happy in having their
families with them are Mrs. Chilton and her sweet
daughter, Mary, who has ever a special attendant
in the person of one of Edward Winslow's brothers
(two of whom had joined him in his life at Leyden
and preparations for this adventure), so her valuable bundles of baggage are well looked after in their
transportation into the ship.

All is well too, in the heart of Elizabeth Tilly,
whose father is more than half her world, and next
in it, the object of her girlish admiration, Desire
Minter — the ward of lovely Mrs. Carver. Her step-

mother and uncle's family are all part of the out-
going company also, so her spirits may be light
enough to amuse the children — herself but little
past the boundaries of their land — Elizabeth Tilly
with sparkling eyes and wind-blown hair, as we see
her then, child of mystery and of argument after
centuries have gone. Doubtless any or all of the
older members of that company could have answered
a question that still burns for some of us — who was
her mother? Why the airy tradition floating down
the years that she was grand-daughter of John
Carver? As much, that, at one time, seemed un-
fathomable, has come to light regarding these people,
this question may one day be definitely answered.

Katherine Carver and Elizabeth Winslow, feeling
that since their husbands believed in this venture,
and since they could make new and comfortable
homes for them anywhere, all was well, are anxious
to be off, especially as the former had for some
time been separated from her husband, and looked
forward to seeing him soon, at Southampton, where
he was to meet their ship. Also the wife of Captain
Standish, who had joined this expedition, thought
that any undertaking with which her martial husband connected himself was right, and so long as she
could be with him in any part of the world, happiness would be hers. These three women, having only
their husbands to think of, are naturally drawn
together, and each can appreciate the beauty and
charm of the others, being equally lovely herself.

Like Mary Chilton and her mother, Priscilla

Mullins and her's are happy in the thought that they are not to be separated from one another nor from the men of their family.

Among the friends of all these women accompanying them from Leyden, for the sweet sorrow of parting, is Juliana Morton, sole representative of the Carpenter family, whose daughters had been gay companions with them all, in past days. Juliana and her husband and family alone remained in Leyden, to this date, and for a time thereafter. The parents and the two younger sisters, Mary and Priscilla, returned to their old home in England; Agnes Fuller slept under the shadow of St. Peter's church and Alice Southworth with her husband and two boys were at this time living in London — business affairs of Edward Southworth having shortened their stay in Leyden. They, however, were thoroughly in touch with the plans of their old friends, and knew of the difficulties with which they had contended. They also knew of the preparations being made for another ship with passengers, some of them strangers, some friends, to sail from London to meet the ship from Delfshaven, at Southampton, and together cross the ocean. Like others of the original company their affairs did not admit of themselves being voyagers at this time.

Sarah Fletcher and Hester Cooke are two others whose hearts we feel are heavy, as their husbands are to precede them to a new country, and they must remain with all the others who will await the first opportunity to follow.

The tide has come in, the wind is fair. Now gaily clad sailors are getting up anchor on the little ship, filled with those whose trust is in her. All ashore for those not going — the last, the very last farewells must be said. Their beloved pastor once more leads them all in prayer, his entire flock about him for the last time. And so they "took their leave one of another; which proved to be the last leave to many of them."

The ship moves out from the wharf, the wind shakes the flag — their English flag — above them, token of their regained nationality. A volly of shot from shore and three guns fired from the ship echo over the watchers waving to each other as long as individuals may be distinguished, and longer. How eagerly the imagination pictures the scene. The *Speedwell* on that fair summer morning, sails into the unseen fog of disappointment and failure that shall prove her name a sad mistake. But for all on board of her "the fire of their faith lights the sea and the shore."

So they leave forever, Holland, that refuge which for twelve years had sheltered them, that school wherein they have been shaped and prepared for the great enterprise before them. Their own country's flag above them, their own little vessel to carry them once more to England, if only for a farewell. Thus the spirits of sadness and expectation attend them and of gratitude and hope.

The summer breezes blowing from England's

shores came out to meet the little ship and caressed the hair and cheeks of that group of England's daughters who stood, drawing their long cloaks about them, on the deck of the *Speedwell* as it entered Southampton water. Once more, as so often in their dreams these past years, they behold their native land. An interlude of vision. Only two of them will ever return; for the rest it will remain a dream, a memory — for "Memory draws from delight ere it dies an essence that breathes of it many a year."

An animated day this proves to be, with greetings from old friends and new acquaintances who have come in the ship from London to join them. The ship! They view it riding at anchor. Of its name or history few of them care. Yet what other ship has held more truly the form of fate for its passengers and of epoch for the world! But they could not know and it seemed then only their guide to cross the sea, their means of accomplishing the only way out of their difficulties.

A company of shrewd business men, as profiteering a syndicate as ever crushed the individual, had happened on this ship at the time they needed one of its size and accommodations for the enterprise they were planning to undertake in sending a homeless, well-nigh friendless, but dauntless company of men and women to colonize in America, chiefly on the money of these same people but supplemented by some of their own, and many directions, conditions and restrictions for their endeavors to which

they had reluctantly to agree. King nor country
cared, the merchants, their nominal backers, cared
less than nothing for the personal success or good
fortune of these voyagers, except only where advancement of their own selfish interests or claims
for territorial advantage accrued and might be returned.

These two boat loads of pioneers regarded thus
with indifference, may be viewed for a moment in
contrast to that subsequent fleet of English ships
carrying English passengers on whom all England
from Crown to Commons looked with interest and
in whom hope and pride were centered — the ships
bearing colonists under the leadership of John
Winthrop, to the same shores, ten years later,
saluted by royal guns as they sailed away as voyagers whose adventure would reflect honor and
renown to the kingdom, whose loss would be a
disaster to the nation, while if either or both of these
two unimportant ships with all on board had sunk
at sea, as so nearly happened, the incident would not
have seemed worth recording for a paragraph of
history by the country, who treated these loving
children with contempt and disdain. Nevertheless
these brave pilgrims prepared the way for all others
who later sought homes on the far shores of their
intent and gave them aid and comfort by personal
contact as well as by their example of unfaltering
purpose. For their recompense to the merchants
commercially interested in their adventure, the account shows them more than over-paid, at length.

For their advantage to the country they left forever, since it did not understand them and did not want them, in long, long years from that day, perhaps the arrival of the first contingent of American destroyers in British waters, in the spring of 1917, to give a certain aid and comfort to England, may be accounted a return.

But thoughts like these were not in their minds as they are in ours. The ship from London, by name, *Mayflower,* was before them — an actuality, while for us it is a vision.

This vessel was twice the size of the little *Speedwell* and bore a popular and one of the oldest names for British ships. A predecessor of the name had in 1415 borne the flower of knighthood to France, to fight at Agincourt. Another had been flagship of the Duke of Gloucester. *This Mayflower* had already a noteworthy career, the equal, of any, as a warship. She had been a member of Queen Elizabeth's fleet, contributed to it by a city guild, and took a brilliant and prominent part in the fights of the Spanish Armada to the final, desperate and victorious one. Nevertheless in spite of this, her name would not have gilded a page in history, but on the day she sailed from London for Southampton, equipped for a long voyage across the sea, destiny began to weave for her the wreath of fame. Not a large ship — 120 or more tons — and about 82 feet long, but what other is greater? Which more inspiring to poets and artists? The true and accepted model of the *Mayflower* is on exhibition at the National Museum in Washington, this was made by Capt. J. W. Collins, an expert in naval architecture, by order of the United States Government.

At Southampton the companies of each ship mingled on shore and on shipboard while the vessels were being made ready for departure. The allotments to the respective ships, the designation of quarters in the ships, were necessarily made chiefly with regard to the needs and comfort of the women and children. The number of each was increased by the wife and family of Stephen Hopkins and of John Billington, also by four children named More. These children, three boys and a girl, were protegees of Mr. Weston, one of the merchants interested, and, having no apparent connection with any one of the company; just what reason he had for sending them on this voyage seems likely to remain an unanswered question. The loving natures of Mary Brewster, Katherine Carver and Elizabeth Winslow accepted them as their special charges, and Jasper was thereafter considered with the numerous and varied family of the Carvers, Ellen, with the Winslows, while Richard and his other brother, increased the Brewster's number of boys. For only a short time were these children to know these new and kind friends. Another unexpected addition to their numbers was in the person of the young man of Southampton, John Alden by name, who joined their company, as cooper, for the sake of the voyage and adventure — but who remained as one of them for the sake of the love and admiration he gained for some in particular. Their business affairs being concluded, the *Speedwell* and *Mayflower* sailed from the harbor, but soon the *Speedwell* was found in a dangerous condition from leaks,— though she had been thoroughly overhauled after her trip from Holland. It was decided to put into the nearby port of Dartmouth, where a stay was made of ten days, at much cost to the pilgrims both in time and money. However, after this set-back, the ships sailed again and all had hopes of comfortable progress. Land's End was behind them about a hundred leagues on the 23rd of August, when the Captain of the *Speedwell* again proclaimed that disaster to his ship was imminent. There was nothing else to do but turn both ships back to the nearest port. Plymouth welcomed them and kind-hearted people there tried to comfort and cheer the disappointed passengers. For some, these several returns to England began to affect their spirits as a portent or warning, but to others they but served to make stronger the desire to carry out their plans, in spite of discouragement, in spite of the charm of England's summer days beside the sea, in spite of the bright and friendly town through whose massive gateways they had to pass to visit the busy streets and get their last glimpses of gay shops — sights which they realized they would never again see when they had emigrated to the new and lonely land. This acid test lasted fourteen days.

About this time, in their house in Dukes's place, Edward and Alice Southworth received a letter

written by Robert Cushman, while at Dartmouth,
relating the unpleasant events that had transpired.
Their sympathies were doubtless awakened, but even
more their surprise, when, not long after, Robert
and Mary Cushman and their son, returned to London; they and a number of others both from choice
and necessity had left the company at Plymouth
when it was finally decided to abandon the thought
of the *Speedwell* making the voyage and that the
Mayflower would go on alone.

Such of the passengers who had come from Leyden
and who were to continue their voyage, were trans-
ferred with their effects to the other ship, and in this
unexpected turn of their affairs, all had to make
themselves as comfortable as possible. Disappointment and the discouraging delay could not have lent
much enthusiasm to the re-arranging of themselves
and their family belongings, especially in such
crowded quarters as now became necessary. Finally,
all being adjusted, the *Speedwell* sailed for London
and the *Mayflower* for her long voyage.

Compactness could never have had a more effec-
tive demonstration, when one considers what actually was required by these colonists in the way of
equipment, the number of people and the size of
the ship. Though the Leyden contingent had brought
little more than personal belongings, and as few as
possible, the *Speedwell* had little spare space, while
on board the *Mayflower* when she sailed from London
were not only the passengers and their accessories,
but supplies for the enterprise as a whole — other

necessaries being added at Southampton — also the
regular ship's supplies for the vessel and crew for
a long voyage and return.

Let us glance at a list of articles which we know
were part of the load: building materials for houses
and boats, clothing materials, beds and bedding,
rugs, spinning-wheels, chairs, chests, cradles, cooking utensils, carpentering tools, books, weapons,
gunpowder and shot, cannon, garden and farm im-
plements, seeds and plants, medicines, trinkets for
trading with the Indians, goats, chickens, pigs,
pigeons, dogs, beer and butter, food for the animals,
dried and salted foods for the people. And some of
these things we may see this day, as they have been
seen on any day of these three hundred years since
they were shipped on the *Mayflower*.

We have heard careless or would-be witty remarks
as to the countless china tea pots, which came in the
Mayflower and are in every state in the Union, or
household furnishings which would supply largely
populated cities by the number claimed as authentic.
Such amusing remarks cause a smile indeed, not
however, from the cause the sarcastic authors as-
sume, but from the ignorance or exaggeration willingly or unconsciously evinced. The known freight
the *Mayflower* carried was a ship load and no more
— and some of it remains to the present hour.
China tea pots, or even one, never was part of her
invoice; tea and coffee were not then known as
beverages to these people, nor in their world; what
a solace and comfort therefore was missing for the

women of the voyage — for at sea, how seemingly indispensable are these important factors of present day life.

The women of the *Mayflower* — let us look at them now, since all who ever may be called by that name are together on the ship, and fair days and moonlight nights give possible encouragement to them as the voyage opens. We see the forms of those we have known in England and Leyden, heretofore, some more familiar to us than others, but we are interested in all, however slight our acquaintance; and their new companions, lately from London, claim our attention likewise. Among these latter we note Mrs. Stephen Hopkins as an addition of great advantage; her vigor of mind and body, her decidedly wholesome and attractive personality wins regard from all. Her own little daughter, Damaris, and her step-daughter, Constantia, added one each to the quota of childhood and girlhood on board. Against the name of Elizabeth Hopkins, as against the names of two others of the matrons of this passenger list, (Mary Brewster and Susanna White) destiny set a shining mark.

Mrs. John Carver has her maid and her young ward, Desire Minter, also the frequent company of her dear friends, Mrs. Myles Standish and Mrs. Edward Winslow. It needed not for John Carver to be one of the leading men of this company, nor for him and his wife to have more of worldly goods than many, for Katherine Carver to have the love and admiration of all who knew her.

Quite a stranger to all is Mrs. Christopher Martin,
and scarcely known during her brief stay among
them; she and her husband were among the passengers from London.

Two pairs of mothers and daughters, — Mrs.
Chilton and Mary, Mrs. Mullins and Priscilla —
engage our attention, as Cupid's entanglements are
even in this serious adventure, since Mary has lost
an admirer and Priscilla gained one. There was not
room for both of Edward Winslow's brothers on
the larger ship, when the *Speedwell* failed their
hopes, so John had to seek the new world and his
winsome Mary, at a later day. John Alden, the
young cooper, engaged for the voyage at Southampton, has already met his fate in acquaintance with
the buoyant Priscilla. The names of these two sweet
maids of the *Mayflower*, (soon to become sorrow-
touched women of the new colony) ripple as music
through poetry and romance, or staid fact and history to our imagination.

Here is a group whom we know far less well; Mrs.
Thomas Tinker, Mrs. John Rigdale, Mrs. Francis
Eaton, yet we feel sure their qualities of mind and
heart must be the equal of many of their companions.

Here are the sisters-in-law, wives of John and
Edward Tilly, each with a young girl to mother —
not her own — for Humility Cooper is cousin to
Ann Tilly, and Elizabeth is a step-child to John
Tilly's wife.

Mrs. Edward Fuller, sister-in-law of the doctor

and Anna White, is one of those sailing for another
haven than some of the others, though knowing it
not.

From London has come Mrs. John Billington, so
different in style and manner from her women companions as to be quite noticeable, yet not lacking
in desirable qualities to say the least; and little
Ellen More, now in Mrs. Winslow's care.

Mrs. William Bradford — standing in the shadow
of tragedy — and Mrs. Isaac Allerton with her two
little girls, Remember and Mary, complete the
count. Mary Allerton's namesake daughter stands
nearest to us, of all that company, between that day
and this.

> "How slow yon tiny vessel plows the main!
> Amid the heavy billows now she seems
> A toiling atom — then from wave to wave
> Leaps madly, by the tempest lashed, — or reels,
> Half wrecked, through gulfs profound.
> Moons wax and wane,
> But still that lonely traveller treads the deep."

What words can better picture the *Mayflower* at
sea than these of Mrs. Sigourney? The monotony,
the discomfort, the terrors day after day. Since the
waning of the September moon, under which the
voyage began, the weather had become cold and
stormy; the sea dangerous — whose roughness affected many and made the labors and duties of those
able to withstand it, increase.

The ship's cook was of slight service to the passengers, since his work was for the benefit of the

officers and crew only, therefore the preparing of their meals fell to the different individuals whose health and abilities so enabled them. With slight cooking facilities, it was necessary to rely chiefly upon such fare as did not require to be prepared by fire; gin and brandy were relied upon for warmth, and beer a tonic.

To this tossing ship, on one of these stormy days, there comes a stranger, promptly and appropriately called Oceanus, and the Hopkins family becomes one of especial interest, with its new baby for all the women and children to delight in.

Another day's excitement is provided by one of the young men, who chafing under the restraint of staying below decks, imposed by the storm, ventures above and is no sooner out than over the side of the ship, in the grip of a wave. His presence of mind to grasp a rope, which trailed from the rigging in the water and his grit in holding on, making his rescue possible by the sailors, make a topic of conversation with sufficient thrill. One wonders if John Howland became invested with a new interest for Elizabeth Tilly from that day, or the few subsequent ones, when the great, hearty fellow was somewhat the worse for his adventure.

The shock of death enters when a particularly rough sailor, who had terrorized the women and children and annoyed the men by his language and manners, is stricken suddenly, buried at sea, and so one of their trials is removed.

The storm increases and all doubt not that their

end is approaching, since the ship is giving way, but
this crisis passes, by the energies of the captain and
crew and the aid of an iron screw, or jack, which
was brought by a passenger from Leyden. That
screw was the instrument which saved the *Mayflower,* and we know not the owner — whose name
seems of more interest to us than it did to them to
whom the screw was the thing.

Another day brings a blow to Doctor Fuller and
to all, since one of their own company is summoned
by death, the young assistant to the doctor, William
Button. Many begin to show the effects of the
dreary weeks on the ship and look worn, weary and
ill.

At last, at last, in a November dawn, land is in
sight! A day spent in running southward looking
for a favorable harbor, but none appearing, they
turn about and return to the point of land first
seen, and by nightfall are safely riding at anchor.

With the episode immediately following, the
women had no actual connection, yet to some we
know it was of interest, as their husbands signed
the document drawn up in the cabin, and because
of it Katherine Carver was made the "first lady"
of the little group of friends, since her husband was
then duly elected governor of this colonial company.
More love, more respect, they could not give her as
their governor's wife than they had always given
her as just one of themselves — tested and trained
as all had been together in the years of friendship
amid all the shades of mutual experience.

The next day new life and animation was evident among all on board the *Mayflower*. Hope flung aside the grey veils that had almost enveloped her for many weeks and stood in the radiant garments of expectancy — they would not recognize the vagueness, the emptiness of her background. They had been brought across the sea in safety — they were about to disembark on the solid ground of their new country. Ambition stirred the weakest to prove the wisdom of their choice.

In the cabin of the *Mayflower*, next day, their Elder led them in prayer and hymns of thankfulness. Around were those who had listened to him in the old hall at Scrooby Manor, and others who, since then, had made his way their way through life. We may easily picture, again, Mary, his devoted wife, seated in the old chair (which, at least, we may see actually), her gentle, anxious face silhouetted against the grim old cabin walls of the *Mayflower*, as lovely to her friends who looked at her that day, as when its fairness had as a background her old home in the stately manor in England. All who were able were at this service, on what, for them, was Expectation Sunday, (though some were too weak and ill to leave their berths), and afterwards, walked on the decks looking at the new, mysterious land before them — recognizing various familiar trees, growing almost to the water's edge, and accepting the attention of the surprised but welcoming sea-gulls. The little pool, across a stretch of nearby beach, partly surrounded by juniper trees, attracted the eyes of the women with delight at prospect, if tomorrow was fair, for a grand and general wash day, with plenty of water, instead of the restricted supply that had had to suffice them for more than a hundred days' effort at cleanliness.

The cold, foggy morning of the 23rd of November witnessed much energy among the company on the ship, riding at anchor in its lonely harbor. Small boats brought many of the women ashore with kettles and big bundles, — the first time that they set foot on the soil of their new country—and Monday wash day was established. The men who were not employed repairing the small boat, or shallop, which had been stored in the hold of the *Mayflower*, and which they wished to use for exploration as soon as possible, cut the fragrant cedars or junipers about the pool, made cheerful, pungent fires, and swung the kettles for the boiling water. Some, no doubt, looked on it as quite a picnic, with lunch served by the fire, and the whole thing a change from the life of the past weeks.

The dusk saw the footprints of many English women marking for the first time that sea-washed shore, and the ashes of the first fires of civilized life, (with women as an important half of that life), mingling with the sands. The women went "home" to the ship, with contentment in their minds, but wet, cold and tired. Small wonder that colds became evident next day — with little vitality left to resist them. Misery had plenty of company.

Another day and the anxious wives whose husbands made up the first exploring party watched them row away in the ship's long boat, land and march along the shore, out of sight, under the watchful lead of Captain Myles Standish.

Through the two days and nights of their absence, knowing not what dangers or disasters might befall them, we can never doubt that the secret prayers of Rose Standish unceasingly appealed for the safe return of her husband and the husbands of the other women, her dear friends, for whom he was responsible. And not her's only we know were answered, when, on the third morning, the welcome sound of guns from shore, signaling the long boat, relieved the tension on the ship. What rejoicing, interest and even amusement was the result of their safe arrival, with curious trophies of their first land journey and descriptions of what they had seen and done.

After a few days, their own shallop being repaired, another and larger party went away for discovery. Another safe return and tales of interest followed this. And news of importance awaited them, also — for they found the White family rejoicing in the arrival of a son and brother; Dr. Fuller and Mr. and Mrs. Edward Fuller in a new nephew, and Samuel in a cousin, in the little Pilgrim. Probably Oceanus Hopkins looked at his future playmate with interest, not unmixed with surprise that he was no longer the new baby of the *Mayflower*.

Before the next attempt to find the place most desirable for their permanent location, another event, far less cheerful, drew attention to the Whites. A young man in their employ, Edward Thompson, died, and thus became the first of the *Mayflower* passengers to be buried in American soil.

The following day, one of the Billington boys in search of diversion, finding a loaded gun in the cabin and a barrel of gunpowder, promptly shot it off then and there; his pleasure was short-lived, but those who were ill or much startled by the noise, probably did not care what happened to him. The jeopardy in which he placed the ship and every soul on board was doubtless beyond his comprehension. The restlessness of the small boys in those cramped quarters was one of the trials the mothers had to bear. Our sympathy is for both.

On the 16th of December, reckoning by the calendar as we know it, the third and, as it proved to be, the final and successful attempt at finding the place for their settlement was made. But while much happened to the exploring party, in the seven days of its absence, and while the thoughts of those left on the ship followed them, at all times, hearts were heaviest there, and gloom as great as that surrounding the storm-tossed shallop settled on the *Mayflower*. The moments were tense to the family of James Chilton, whose illness daily became more acute, and hope of his recovery faded in the hearts of his loving wife and daughter. Into the loving sympathy of their friends and their own deep sorrow, there entered a shock and excitement of stunning effect, when it was discovered that Dorothy

Bradford was missing. Someone had seen her on deck — we see her, too — standing, in the sunset, wrapped in her long cape, looking over the water, alone.

We recall her as, years past, we saw her on another winter afternoon, in Amsterdam, standing with Patience Brewster on the banks of the canal. gay with skaters — the elder's daughter, then, now the wife of one of the principal men of this company.

One who kept a record of those days wrote: "At anchor in Cape Cod harbor. This day Mistress Dorothy Bradford, wife of Master Bradford, who is away with the exploring party, to the westward, fell overboard and was drowned." A woman of the *Mayflower* whose experience of the New World was destined to be brief — and never of Plymouth Colony — the one appointed to lead the way into a New Country for many of the women who sorrowed that night for her sudden going. That no further comment or record was made of this tragedy seems remarkable. Out of the silence conjectures arise, as will in such conditions, without form or foundation in truth as far as can ever be known.

Mr. Chilton died the next day — the first head of a family to be taken. The illness which was gradually affecting many of the company, grew out of the colds and run down condition they had reached. It seems like grip or influenza of our modern knowledge, with other complications; its fatality was appalling. Mary Chilton and her mother had need

of the uplifting sympathy and companionship of
such friends as Mary Brewster and Susanna White
in the dark hours of their sorrow. Theirs was the
first test of faith. The little family of three had
expected to face the new life together, with whatsoever pleasure or privation it might bring, and to
have the one taken for whom and with whom the
other two had willingly ventured, strong in their
love and determination to bear their part in the
work which needed women's hands to secure even
a semblance of home, was crushing indeed. Yet
these women, already proven brave, would now be
braver still and rejoice in the safe return in the
shallop of the other husbands and fathers who
brought the good news of a satisfactory place to
establish their settlement.

The enthusiasm of these men at the happy ending
of their uncomfortable and dangerous journey was
soon lessened by knowledge of the grievous and
unexpected events which had happened while they
were away.

We think it was Elder Brewster who gave the sad
explanation to William Bradford as to why Dorothy
was not with the cluster of women and girls who
crowded so eagerly at the ship's rail to catch first
glimpse of their men as the discoverers returned.
These men had lately seen and touched a rock, for
them a stepping-stone, that day of exploration, to
solid ground — they saw it not as the gateway of a
mighty nation; a rock which had wandered to that
place from far away; a traveller, a pilgrim who had

waited long to welcome these pilgrims. They returned now to the rock of their community, William
Brewster, keystone of the arch of their high aspira-
tions, molder and guardian of the firm principles
that other rock so fitly typified.

One more storm and struggle for the *Mayflower*
on weighing anchor again, one more disappointing
return to a harbor which she desired to leave, but
after all a calm day's sail across the bay and rest
in that quiet harbor guarded by the lonely rock.
Her work nobly performed, her name immortal, she
had reached the goal.

THE FIRST STREET.

THE FIRST STREET.

THE FIRST STREET of Plymouth, the first street of New England, was in the making. From the decks of the *Mayflower* the women looked longingly toward the land, whither the men went daily, hearing the sounds of hammering and sawing which came across the harbor, for as yet none of them had been permitted to go ashore in these new surroundings. The hill which arose at the water's edge, behind the rock, was snow-crowned; around and beside it a path had been cut and worn by the men as they went to the work of making houses for their families.

By the maps and charts of the company, it was found that this situation, which they had all approved for their permanent residence, was the place visited and named by an earlier explorer of whom they had heard, and some had seen, Captain John Smith. The appellation he gave to it suited them well — Plymouth; if they had had the selection of a name as well as the site for their New World home, it could not have been better chosen, in view of the fact that Plymouth was the last place their feet had trod and their eyes seen in their Old World home. and the inhabitants of that town had been kind to them.

Nevertheless it was of Leyden that they thought when building. The larger hill at the end of the street, which they at first saw in the mind's eye, even as we do now, reminded them of the eminence crowned by the fort at Leyden, and upon it they would build their fort and it would be a constant reminder of the Burg.

But first must be built the store-house to hold all their belongings moved from the ship, and then the few houses necessary to shelter themselves. Of these plans they talked at night when the men returned to the ship or on the days when the weather was so inclement that no trip could be made ashore; these delays were a constant strain upon the nerves of all, as the need for haste was so evident, with winter's storms increasing and the impatience of the crew growing therewith, to say nothing of the failing health and strength of so many of themselves.

The fortitude and patience of the women who had braved all the dangers, shared all the trials, and now, in spite of courage and cheerfulness seemed fading before their eyes was enough to urge every man to use his own last reserves of energy and strength to provide better conditions for them. They well realized the important asset to their venture, of the women. Without them not even the magnetism and charm of Brewster, the indomitableness and courage of Myles Standish, the business ability of Allerton, the experience of Hopkins, the worldly wisdom of Winslow, the youth and strength of John Howland and John Alden or the zeal and fervor of Bradford and Carver could have assured the stability and success of this colony. Previous settlements

in this region and others further south bore witness
to a lack of something making for continued interest
and permanence on the part of the men, who were
not wanting in necessary personal qualities. The
abandonment of such ventures in Maine and Virginia, where no women had accompanied the men,
is proof that a common larder and fireside are not
the things for which men struggle against hardship,
disaster and death. But the street of Plymouth,
albeit made in the face of every trial of circumstance, was made by men for the women they loved,
and Plymouth has never been abandoned nor its
street untrod by the families and descendants of
these men and women.

The weeks of January drag by, spent by the men
ashore, many not returning to the ship at night when
the roof of the store-house was finished, both to save
the time of the trip back and forth and to guard
their belongings already there; so lights gleamed at
night from Plymouth, seen by the weary watchers
on the ship and the ship lights shone in the sight
of the builders, signals to one another yet seeming
to make the gloom of their situation more visible.

The violent storm which ushered in the month
caused the *Mayflower* to madly roll and tug at three
anchors necessary to hold her; in the midst of this
discomfort, the third birth occurred on the ship, but
the son of Isaac and Mary Allerton never knew the
world to which he came. One of the young men,

Richard Britteridge, also died about this time, and
so the burials began on the snow-covered hill.

The women had more to do, however, than look
towards the shore and long to land, for the life on
the ship was not an idle one for any of them while
health and strength lasted. As, one by one, illness
attacked them, those remaining well had many
added cares. Assisting Doctor Fuller, attending to
the wants of the families of those mothers who were
ill, preparing the food for the sick and for the men
who went daily ashore to work, keeping the children
safe and amused, and, above all, keeping their own
faith and hope alive went on as unendingly as the
swell of the sea beneath them.

By the end of the month, the house built to store
their belongings and to shelter some of them while
the others were being erected, was finished and was
also a hospital in its capacity of general or common
house, for numbers of the workers had to occupy the
beds as fast as they could be brought from the ship,
their brave fight against the odds overwhelming
many. The women had an hour of frightful suspense when, suddenly, before the eyes of some looking towards the land, flames leapt out and shouts
were heard. They were sure the dreaded event had
happened — that the Indians had attacked and van-
quished all ashore. But the later knowledge that no
Indians had appeared and no one was hurt, recon-
ciled them to the loss of the roof of the common
house from too great a fire in the chimney; it had
to be relaid — and then the joyful decision was made

that all who were able should come from the ship
on the next Sunday for a service in the common
house, which was to serve also as church and bar-
racks for a time.

The little ship of the Pilgrims, called only "the
shallop," and already proven staunch and true to
their needs, leaves the side of the *Mayflower* on this
wintry Sunday, with the women as passengers for
the first time, and sails over the mile or so of water
towards the landing. Some are using their greatest
efforts; some are too weak to come at all, and even
those still well are vastly different in looks and manner from their appearance at leaving old Plymouth
or even on that first Monday of enthusiasm at Cape
Cod. But all feel that a new era is dawning and
again the need calls out the latent spirit of sacrifice
inherent in every woman, on this occasion once more
requiring the putting aside of personal feelings of
sorrow or illness for the common good. From the
day when these women gave up their early associations and left their English homes to live in a
strange country among people with different customs and language, striving to preserve their own
during the twelve years of their sojourn, through
the time of their embarking at Delfshaven and later
sailing from Plymouth, when they saw cherished
possessions and loved members of their families left
behind, during the famous voyage with its heart-
rending conditions for them of wet, cold, poor food,
overcrowding, storms, anxiety, to the day they

landed, worn and exhausted with no homes to go to,
new hardships and dangers awaiting them, self-
sacrifice was in a continually ascending scale and,
for many, could go no further.

Some of the men are standing on the rock, watching the progress of the boat, some are grouped at
the Common House on guard, as ever, against a surprise from the unknown Indians. The governor, the
elder, several of the other men whose wives are in
the boat, two or three of the younger men we may
see in the grave group at the landing, but the light
of expectancy and contentment for this one hour at
least, glows in their faces. With costumes so similar
it is hard to distinguish where each woman is placed
in the shallop and to single out a special one for
whom a man may be looking. At the bow two or
three are grouped, waving to their welcomers, their
alertness seeming to be an urge to the little craft.
The eager children are held from crowding forward
as they near the shore. An instant of excitement,
the sailors making ready to fasten the boat, it
touches, is beside the rock; the woman who stood
foremost at the bow on the way over, has poised herself a second and sprung from the boat, catching at
the outstretched hands of the nearest man, to steady
her foothold on the slippery stone; the keen wind
and spray have dashed color in her cheeks, the brilliancy of sun on snow is reflected in her eyes — a
flashing triumph at being the first — it is Mary
Chilton. Someone has said that Plymouth Rock
began with her its fame, but for her and for the

other women, quickly following her to clasp the hands of the men, — as it had been for those men — it became for them the threshold into Plymouth Colony. Some of the women of the *Mayflower* have not gotten so far, and some of these scarce pass the threshold.

The service is held, as planned; once more they listen to the uplifting and strengthening words of their Elder. Afterwards some return to the *May-flower*, but others remain with their husbands on shore.

The work on the other houses goes forward as rapidly as possible. All were built of squared logs, the crevices filled with clay, the roofs a thatch of the swamp grass, resembling their English cottages in this. The few windows have only oiled paper to resist the winter's storms. Each house is set on a plot of ground of its own on either side of the street — the location for each family being decided by lot. Yet building by men cramped with rheumatism and sciatica, or falling down from weakness as a prelude to illness and death is not a rapid business, and, for all that they planned at first to live as compactly as possible, without being crowded, the unattached young men to be part of the families — as they had been in Leyden — it soon became evident that many houses would not be needed.

In less than a week after the first visit of the women ashore, not all the prowess of Myles Standish, hero of war in Flanders, not all his own unending strength and endurance, could defend his Rose from

the blight of illness nor shield his heart from the
sharp stab of sorrow. She had dreamed of the new
home in a land of fair skies, sunshine and flowers,
not this region of snows; she knew how thin and
white she was growing, but she knew that her husband had not ventured on any vain purpose, and
willed to be brave for his sake. Her high resolves
were not long tested however, ere she gained the
reward of her faith.

Others soon followed her, and, having but crossed
the threshold, Ann Tilly, Mrs. Martin, little Ellen
More and Mary Chilton's mother were gone from the
colony; another month and Mary Allerton, John
Tilly's wife, Sarah Eaton and the sister-in-law of
Doctor Fuller (Mrs. Edward Fuller), were num-
bered with them. Meanwhile, Susanna White had
become a widow, and Elizabeth Tilly an orphan,
with Mary Chilton, and soon Priscilla Mullins was
added to these girls' forlorn state. Alice Rigdale
and her husband; Thomas Tinker, his wife and
child, needed not houses nor land in Plymouth. Two
of the More boys and a number of the young men
fell victims in the great mortality, and Sarah Priest,
in Leyden, was a widow, though nearly a year
passed before she knew it. A little later and Elizabeth Winslow slipped from the gentle hand clasp
of Katherine Carver, to join her other dear friend,
Rose Standish.

Thus twelve wives were swept away by this fatal
epidemic, some from the *Mayflower*, some from the
land. Even the comfort of graves bearing their

names which should tell those who loved them, and others, that they had been with them, was denied them. But their monument is the hill by the seashore, on which their graves were made, and their remembrance shall last as long as mayflowers blossom.

From the time of the first anchoring of the ship (at Cape Cod) of the total of the twenty-five women and young girls, thirteen were released from their labors. It is indeed remarkable that even twelve should have survived. Into the hearts of those recovering from their own illness, the spirit of desolation must have entered for a time, as they struggled to their feet again, to grieve for those who were laid to rest under the snow and to take up the burdens of life once more. Many of the men had gone, too, but few of the children.

For the five elder women, life, even under the circumstances, still was worth while. The governor's wife had the loving care and interest of all but two of her household's original numbers; her husband, her young ward, her maid and John Howland; two of the other young men, as well as the little boy she cared for on the voyage, Jasper More, had gone. But deepest grief was not, as yet, her portion. Mary Brewster, too, was strengthened by the sight of her husband untouched by illness and apparently not weakened by the terrific work and strain he had been under, and her own two boys, soon helping as ably as before, and even Richard More, the sole survivor of his family, was already one of her's. For Eliza-

beth Hopkins and Eleanor Billington not one of
their own particular groups were gone. But
Susanna White had left only her own two children,
her nephew and her brother—and he, of course,
seemed to belong to each one as much as to her.

Humility Cooper and Elizabeth Tilly, Priscilla
Mullins and Mary Chilton were indeed the most
truly alone, each one being the sole representative of
her family.

On the five women the care and responsibility fell
heaviest, though the girls and even the children had
their share in the general division of labor. Each
served while there was nursing to be done. Cooking
was not only a duty but a serious problem in finding
the wherewithal to tempt failing appetites or keep
up the strength of the men and children. Who can
doubt that these women often went hungry that others might have more? Scarce wonderful that Mary
Brewster and Katherine Carver never regained their
full health again. The former took to her home and
mother love the homeless and motherless girls, sadly
missing her own daughters, so far away.

Gradually came a lessening of the strain of apprehension of unknown evils; the problem of the
Indians had been solved on the day that they heard
the word "welcome" from a strange voice, and, from
then on, mutual fear diminished between their im-
mediate neighbors in the forest and themselves, and
visits from these strange people became frequent and
helpful as well.

The day of the making of another covenant was

one marked by color and animation in the doleful monotony of those early months, for the women with strength enough for interest. Their governor, with all the formalities of his office, met and entertained the sovereign of the savages, and the lively music of the drum and trumpet, the firm footsteps of the military guard quickened their spirits and brought a sense of assurance. The green rug, on which royalty sat, in one of the unfinished houses, must always have brought back, to the woman who owned it, that scene and its results — the lasting treaty of mutual friendship and benefit. That other rug of modern times, on which the Liberty Bell rested at the Panama-Pacific Exposition, in 1915, afterwards used at celebrations connected with the great generals of the World War, is interesting but not more important in the historical part it has played than the rug which we now see in fancy.

Also their defense from their fort was accomplished, the cannon being landed and dragged up the greater hill, to the summit, and a strong building erected there. Military preparedness began as soon as the men were able to drill, under command of Myles Standish, their chosen Captain.

Gradually, also, Spring came, the children found arbutus and other early flowers, and were happy, though their search might not take them far from sound of the home voices, as the fearsome sound of the wolves was a constant warning. Remember and Mary Allerton and Damaris Hopkins played on the beach with Constance, Elizabeth and Humility, and gathered the bright shells in the warm sunshine till the pink of the shells and arbutus was reflected in their cheeks. The sailors, now that the connection between them and their erstwhile passengers was soon to end and their roughness softened by the common ills of the winter, were glad to tell tales to amuse the children, when lingering ashore.

And, so, with the April mildness on land and sea, came the last night when the lights of the *Mayflower* shone to them out of the darkness. On the morning of its departure, how visible the scene is to us. The women watch from places of vantage, in groups or singly, in company with some men or with the children clinging to them, from the hill beside the street, their wistful eyes following the battered sails out of the harbor, while the guns from the Fort ring out in parting salute the farewell to their ever-ready shelter, to the only connecting link between them and the rest of their race. Each one has been asked a question all have had plenty of time to consider well, if it were needed to repeat, "shall we, shall I go back?" Away with the *Mayflower* to a once familiar life from unfamiliar trials, from haunting memories to friends or relatives left on the other side of the sea? Each woman for herself has answered "No." The venture made in faith by those loved and gone from their sight, should not have been made in vain; the standard formed of high hope and courage should not go down while they were able in the light of that faith and remembrance to carry it forward.

Now only as a mirage can their ship be seen on the far horizon.

Susanna White, clasping her baby closer, stands near the place on the hill where the body of William, her husband, had been laid; not far away near the grave of Elizabeth, his wife, is Edward Winslow. Their eyes, though seeing each other, are viewing things far away. (Could a breath from the lindens of Leyden be wafted to them?) In that moment arose a consciousness of an unfelt emotion — hitherto drowned by selfishness in sorrow — pity.

Mutual shock and endurance was to continue for them all on this same day. To shake from them any idle reflections, the men worked steadily and vigorously for the remaining hours, on the new fields and planting of seeds, the elder, the doctor, the governor, each exerting every energy, as well as the other men and boys. The day proved unusually hot and the governor seemed to feel it greatly. Reaching his home, he lay down to rest, but while his family waited upon him in deep concern, he lost consciousness. Thus not only was the harbor dark that night, but a cloud hung over Plymouth and common anxiety on their governor's account caused the departure of the *Mayflower* to be almost forgotten. But the governor was worn out, not with that day's labor but by his labors, as has been said, ''in three countries and on the sea, as counselor, agent, nurse, farmer, magistrate and man of God,'' and, in spite of their efforts and distress, consciousness did not

return ere he passed from them. In the pathetic
description, by his successor, "he was buried in the
best manner they could, with some vollies of shot
by all that bore arms," and his grave left smooth
and unmarked, as the others on the hill, that it
might not appear to any enemy that their numbers
were lessened. Though the office of governor was
filled, the first lady of the colony had no successor,
since the widower, William Bradford, was chosen.
Her anguish of grief was so intense, and her frail-
ness grew so perceptably, that it became evident her
stay with them was but transitory.

And again, as in Leyden, the doctor's sister kept
the home for him; but there were more members in
the family than in those by-gone days, for Susanna
had three little lads to care for now, and the doctor
three small nephews to play with. Let us follow the
bright rays of the sunset into their cottage on a May
evening. Supper is over, and now is little Peregrine's bedtime. His mother is gently rocking the
cradle, as she mends his brother's stockings, glanc-
ing now and then at the smiling but sleepy baby
and urging him in softest baby language to accom-
pany the "sandman" without further delay; but
Peregrine's ambition seems to be to stay awake on
this bright particular evening and he coos and
laughs in response to his mother's admonitions. His
brother and cousin are romping just outside the
front door and Resolved runs in to get the cane that
had been his father's, to play horse with. Susanna

sits on a bench beneath the little square window, which swings open with its paper pane, and the breeze which enters plays with the soft, curly tendrils of her hair; beside her on the bench stands the little chest of drawers which has ever held her sewing articles and trinkets since William White gave it to her when they were married. A shadow falls across the light and men's voices come to her as her brother passes with a friend, returning from a stroll to enjoy a smoke by the cottage door. Twilight is fast failing now; the baby is at last asleep; Susanna softly puts away her sewing and goes into the living-room, adjoining, to light a candle at the fire-place; she then stands in the doorway to call in Resolved and Samuel, as she does each evening; she sees her brother and his friend on the doorstep bench, also quite a regular occurrence about this hour, and Edward Winslow rises in his courtly manner to receive her smile of greeting. In the few weeks since the sailing of the *Mayflower,* her pity and sympathy have unconsciously awakened an interest which is now slowly dawning in some wonderment upon her, while for Winslow he had already questioned himself if she would be willing to let him take William White's place, and if, on the other hand, she could fill the vacancy left at his hearth-stone by Elizabeth? He thought he knew the answer to the second question, but for the first sought her reply. That Edward Winslow, talented, aristocratic, of good family and of some wealth, should admire her, pictures Susanna for us almost as plainly as his

painted portrait represents him. We have not the
slight details of her features, but in fancying her
with the light brown hair, blue eyes and pink and
white skin of a young English mother in her twen-
ties, we cannot be far wrong; and for character, the
reflections of her life and times show us that which
certified the regard of all who knew her and gives
her to ours. Her good sense ever caused her acceptance of facts and prompt adjustment of her life to
the conditions imposed upon it by circumstances.
By her intelligence and resourcefulness she was
saved from the dissipation of despondency, devoting
her physical and mental energies to making the best
of the situation in which she found herself. With
courage she contemplated the present and took
thought of and measured the possibilities of the future. Her cheerfulness and adaptibility to the
inevitable in meeting her serious problems won her
a victory over them and greatly increased her own
pleasure in living and unquestionably added to the
pleasure of others. She had had advantages of comfortable circumstances always — more than some and
as much as few of the pilgrim women had; her
brother, her husband, were men of education and
breeding, such also the men of the families of her
nearest friends.

Edward Winslow, doing always the unexpected,
but always pleasing himself, soon found the opportunity of settling the question in his thoughts.
Shortly thereafter Mary Brewster again played con-
fident to a neighbor. When the bans were published

at the next Sunday service, announcing such an item
of interest in the lonely, quiet existence of the community, any surprise was soon dissolved for most,
by their regard for the principals. Before May
was over, the simple ceremony took place, performed
by the governor, as magistrate, as he himself has
recorded, "after the fashion of the Low Countries,"
and the first bride of the colony appears before us.
Anna Fuller whom we first knew in Leyden, there
becoming Susanna White, now changes, as far as
name goes, into the second Mistress Winslow of
Plymouth and before her stretch long years of prosperity. And contentment and happiness? Yes,
such as a woman like her will always seek and find.

Natural curiosity ever alert at a time of a wedding
is sadly checked for us, by dearth of description or
detail of this one, so full of an unusual interest. The
old friend Mary Brewster, was surely witness for
the bride, and her brother, the doctor; while the
elder, as properly, was witness for the groom, and
Isaac Allerton, doubtless, as assistant. But what
repast Mary Chilton, Priscilla Mullins and Elizabeth Tilly, reinforced by the culinary skill of Mistress Hopkins, prepared for the newly married
couple, or who were of the wedding guests who partook, or whether at her house or his, we have no
record. We know simplicity was the keynote, as
complying both with the Pilgrim opinion and the
necessity caused by conditions. It was an important
day for the bride and for the young girls, who were
gladly stirred by the event into a remembrance of

romance and a brighter side of life, forgotten for
many a day. It even aroused Katherine Carver
from her lethargy of grief into a wondering attention when Elizabeth Tilly gave to Desire Minter all
the details in her possession, which we gladly would
glean also, if we could. However, the date appears
upon the page of Plymouth history like an illumin-
ated initial letter, for it marks the beginning of a
more normal life. The dark days since their arrival
which seemed emphasized only by sickness and death
and hunger and cold, had passed.

The summer thus ushered in, brought its herbs
for salad and medicine, its wild fruits and berries
of many varieties, its fish and game, also roses to
gladden their eyes, fragrant and colorful, and, owing to the friendliness and good understanding with
the Indians, the colonists might walk in the woods
round about their homes as in the highways of
England.   The two Indians called Squanto and
Hobomok, who attached themselves permanently to
the colony, showed them many things of advantage
in the way of agriculture and home crafts which the
women were as glad to learn as the men.

About six weeks after their marriage, Susanna
Winslow bade her husband the first of the many
farewells she would experience in the coming days,
because of his frequent journeys in the cause of the
colony. He was now to seek the great Indian chief.
Massasoit, with whom the treaty had been made, a
few months before, and the governor had selected
him and Stephen Hopkins for this necessary visit.

The walk through the woods was long and tiresome and consumed more than a week, but the object of their journey was accomplished. Susanna Winslow and Elizabeth Hopkins, awaiting in some natural anxiety at home for their return, or news of them, must have been somewhat startled the day the governor sent them the message he had just received by an Indian runner, that their husbands were nearly starving and struggling homeward, exhausted. These two wives hastily despatched food by the Indian, to meet them at a certain place, and had an abundant supper in readiness on the rainy evening of their return.

Soon after this, the upsetting occurrence of a lost child came upon them, and Eleanor Billington had the sympathy of the mothers because one of her boys had been too venturesome in the woods and strayed away. He was found by the Indians miles from Plymouth and word being brought of this, the governor sent a boat to the place of the Indian encampment which brought the boy back, no worse for his adventure, so this excitement passed. Expeditions among the Indians became necessary, both of forceful and peaceful intent, which made recurring anxiety for the women, until the men had safely returned.

At the close of the summer, once again sorrow filled their hearts, as one more of their number went from the friends who loved her. It was the only happiness left for Katherine Carver to follow her husband out of this world, which no longer con-

tained anything of interest to her and the future no
hope strong enough to relieve her broken heart. So,
lovely and lamented, she was laid to rest on the hill
by the shore, where so many others of their brave
and fair were sleeping. This left but two of the
married women who had left Leyden together:
Mary Brewster and Susanna Winslow. But the
number of the girls remained complete.

The first anniversary of their sailing from old
Plymouth, came and went. The survivors of that
day's company on the ship must have observed it
with many thoughts. These September days were
busy ones, indeed, as preparations to meet the coming winter began. Their Spring planting had been
successful in all except peas, and their harvest of
corn was abundant. The wild grapes were made
into wine, the corn pounded into meal, each household a veritable hive of workers; while the wear and
tear on their clothes must be repaired and new garments made, or purchased when strictly necessary,
from the supply stored in the Common House.

But an interval occurred in this routine and it
may be introduced to us by a picture of the living-
room in the Brewster house, by candle light, which
contains all the women of the colony in earnest dis-
cussion. This conclave is caused by the recent suggestion of the governor that in view of the fact of
their successful harvest, and renewed health, a
period of recreation should be planned and enjoyed
by all; games, feasting, mirth and frolic, a combina-

tion of festivities of both England and Holland
with which they were familiar, and not only were
preparations to be for themselves but for guests —
Chief Massasoit and many of his warriors were to
be invited, with no doubt at all of their acceptance.
Many of the men had been hunting that day to provide the game, and the results were enough to last
a week. It was not questions of what to provide,
but how much of everything would be needed, and
which of them would prepare and roast the wild
turkeys, who boil the fish, who make sauces and side
dishes or cook vegetables, who bake, who make the
salads, and all the other necessary plans for cooks
who are hostesses, and hostesses who are cooks. The
problem has a familiar appearance to many of us
in our own day. Favorite receipts were compared,
and whoever excelled in a certain thing was to have
charge of that supply. All were good cooks so it
was a case of friendly emulation and rivalry in this
novel experience, with which each housekeeper retired that night, after they had talked and planned
to their satisfaction. More than a hundred to be
provided for over a three day period, and eleven
women and young girls to see it through; even the
littlest girls, Remember and Mary Allerton and
Damaris Hopkins had to help, and of course the
men did their share in keeping the great fires burn-
ing and dressing the game, and the boys in carrying
water from the brook. Every iron kettle, every long
and short legged pot and pan, every wooden bowl
and leathern bottle, every pewter dish, with hooks,

spits and trivets were in use; wooden cups or gourds to drink from, and knives and napkins. The only forks were the long-handled iron ones for cooking purposes, their use for the table was not known, their service was supplied by napkins and spoons.

The Indians arrived and encamped around the street, thoughtfully bringing a large supply of venison to add to the bill of fare. The cooks and waitresses in whitest of linen caps, kerchiefs and aprons, with short woolen skirts and buckled shoes, had many steps to take to serve the banqueters seated at the great tables erected in front of the houses; and when the men were having their contests of shooting or games, they cleared away or looked on at the entertainment as they could. They and the children, in sampling the products of their cooking or taking a mouthful, now and then, were kept from being hungry in the midst of plenty by being too busy to eat.

The long shadows of the third day saw the end of the event. And was the first American "block party" a success? We may say that it was. And were the women tired? We will agree to that also. But the men were pleased, the children happy, and one recovers quickly from the fatigue of gratifying achievement. Thus was their public thanksgiving celebrated, by order of the governor.

On a November day some weeks later, household tasks were going as usual; many of the men were gathering the last of the harvest, others getting in the winter's supply of wood. We may see Mistress

Brewster in her kitchen distilling herbs and witch-hazel for domestic medicines, as was the custom of each housewife, that Dr. Fuller's supply might not be too freely drained. She has the help and company of Mary Chilton this afternoon — both unconscious of any special interest that the day may bring to them especially, before its close, yet the unexpected was as often happening then as now. Priscilla and Elizabeth had taken Desire Minter on a search for more sassafras, hoping to entertain and amuse the listless girl, who, since Mrs. Carver's death, seemed to grow each day more unhappy. The two Marys are talking of the return voyage of the *Mayflower* — how long it might have been or how short — and if their friends in England and Holland had received the many letters and messages taken back by the Captain. Suddenly they are startled by the sound of the gun from the fort! Another shot! They are in the street now and likewise every woman and child — it is the signal for assembly — and the men may be seen hurrying from the woods and fields. The Governor accompanied by the Captain and an Indian runner are rapidly descending the hill from the fort, both looking especially determined. The news is soon in possession of all. A ship has entered Cape Cod harbor — seen by the Indians and word brought at once to Plymouth! Surprise and suspense were but some of the feelings this news aroused. They had been seven months without sight or sound of the world beyond their little settlement and its woodland neighbors.

It would have to be Spring before a friendly ship could be expected to find them (for newcomers could not live in comfort or be of use till then) and as England and France were on far from friendly terms, this might be a ship of the latter nationality, seeking them with hostile intent. But preparedness was ever their daily thought and ability to cope with any emergency. Thus the Captain's little army of defense, twenty men, was soon marshalled and ready — none without a gun in hand — to protect their women, children and homes to the last man.

Mary Brewster sees her husband in the front rank, of course. He can fight as ardently as pray, if necessary, and while wishing that an enemy might be converted and enjoy life, if that were impossible, then no question of who should fire first. The Captain had no weaklings in his command, even the boys and younger men were heroes with such leaders. Their eyes sharpened by expectancy and uncertainty, soon discern the stranger's sails, even as the lookout from the fort calls out the fact that it is in view. Intently they wait and watch, when, behold, before their astonished eyes, the flag of England is flung out in greeting! Relief and amazement run a race in their minds. The ship is smaller than the *Speedwell*. The first boat puts out, making straight for the men drawn up on the seashore. In their incredulity they can scarce recognize, can scarce believe, what they see: Robert Cushman grasping the hands of Brewster and Bradford; John Winslow seizing his brother Gilbert's shoulders; Jonathan

Brewster being sprung upon by his brothers, from the ranks, and then Thomas Prence just behind him.

Such confusion and laughter, such embraces and tears of joy as the women, realizing the situation, come running down the street to meet the crowd coming from the water's edge.

And in another boat come two women, friends from Leyden, the widow Ford and her children and Mistress Basset. The relief of the newcomers was quite equal to that of the Plymouth people, but for a different reason. Not finding any signs of habitation in the first harbor of their search, they feared that all survivors had died or been killed by Indians, and as in their long voyage of four months they had consumed about all of their provisions, they feared starvation for themselves. All were in good health, with good appetites and spirits and as soon as their apprehension was dispelled, at sight of their friends and their plentiful supply of food, gaiety reigned. The problem of housing for these thirty-five newcomers was finally settled by nightfall, each housekeeper putting up with some crowding to take in several, and the Common House once more giving shelter. What welcome of friends and relatives, what interest at news from others, the ensuing hours saw; what joyful supper parties that evening!

Thus the isolation of Plymouth was broken. The sails of the *Fortune* had brought them once again the touch of the outside world.

By daylight, another young lady had joined the colony, and Martha Ford opened her eyes, on the

first morning of her life, in Plymouth. Just why
her mother should have come across the ocean at
this time is not clear to us. She was a widow and
evidently of some means to be able to bring all her
children with her. We may suppose, without
stretching the bounds of probability, that her husband had been preparing to bring his family to the
new colony, and that, after his sudden death, she
carried out the plans.

The *Fortune* remained two weeks, and lively
weeks to get her well laden with the first exports of
the colony, furs, lumber and sassafras making a rich
invoice. Letters were written — letters of enthus-
iastic description; letters of encouragement to join
the life of the New World; letters of advice, and letters replying to those received, for many words of
sympathy had been sent in response to the dreary
news brought back by the *Mayflower*. There was a
particular letter from the governor (one of sympathy, also) to Mistress Alice Southworth, in London, since Robert Cushman brought the news of her
recent widowhood.

Robert Cushman had come especially as emissary
from the merchants who had underwritten the Pilgrims, and to see for himself in what condition they
were, for report at home. He was so pleased with
what he experienced, however, that he planned a
permanent stay at a future day, and left his young
son, who had accompanied him, with the governor.

So the *Fortune* was ready to sail, and by her
departure, was to make one more break in the ranks

of the women, since Desire Minter chose to go back in her, to her friends in England, under charge of Robert Cushman. Her health and spirits had so failed that it was considered the best thing for her; thus another blank was made in the life of Elizabeth Tilly, who had found in Desire a dear friend — and in whose heart she was never forgotten. Perhaps Desire already forsaw that her place would soon be taken and knew that she would leave little Elizabeth in good hands. As the *Fortune* sailed out of the harbor, we may see John Howland near Elizabeth with his protective look and ready, encouraging smile.

This little ship did not receive benefit from her name, for fortune proved unkind. A French man-of-war, lying near the coast of England, captured her and took all on board prisoners to a French island, where for more than a fortnight they were detained. However the ship and passengers were then released and reached England — but the valuable cargo and letters were spoils of war. So Alice Southworth never received the governor's letter, but the fact of its having been sent was reported to her by her friend, Robert Cushman. Indeed the various items of news he brought were of interest to many.

But Desire, if she had only written of her experiences, or caused them to be written! Her experiences as a woman of the *Mayflower,* as a woman of Plymouth Colony, her experiences in leaving the latter for an English home — with her war adventure as

an extra detail. What material she had and of what
value for the world to read. She would have been
a rival historian of Bradford and Winslow, for
posterity. But of course such a thought never
occurred to her. She was a woman — and a woman
could not be independent in the society of that day,
which was an exclusively masculine society and with
a system by which feminine conduct was judged
from a masculine point of view. About two hundred
and fifty years elapsed before any other point of
view was deemed possible. And Desire Minter was
far from being the first of her sex to question. In
due time word was brought to Plymouth that she
had reached her friends, and, later on, that her brief,
but not uneventful life was over. Somewhere English roses bloom o'er her grave; an interesting pilgrimage, if its location were known, as a remembrance of the first woman of the *Mayflower* and of
Plymouth Colony to return to her early home.

Meanwhile, before Plymouth knew aught of what
had happened to the *Fortune,* much happened
there. While pleasure in the company of the newcomers lasted, supplies did not, and their bubble of
joy was soon broken. The *Fortune* brought no food,
and thirty-odd extra people, mostly men, to provide
for, was a serious problem. So their second winter
was a hard one to get through, with little to eat —
half rations only — and resultant weakness (though
fortunately no sickness) scarce enabled them to improve their condition. Nevertheless, owing to the
threatening attitude of some of the distant Indians,

a protecting wall of lumber was built around the town. The street ran from the rock to the battlement on the greater hill, but some houses were erected at a different angle which indicated another street for the near future — to be called the Highway — and the square came into view.

In Spring, the women, in addition to household duties, helped plant, the children also — though for them more of a pleasure than for their mothers, struggling with the problems of supply and demand in food and clothes.

On an April day, after the planting, an episode occurred which brings before us for the first time, a woman not hitherto distinctly in the picture. The Indian squaws occasionally came to Plymouth and were a help or a bother, according to their personality, to the women of the colony. One, however, had such agreeable characteristics that she was considered a desirable member of the community. Her husband, Hobomok, was the colony's trusted interpreter and permanent resident. On this day, we see the mothers of the smallest children, Susanna Winslow, Martha Ford and Elizabeth Hopkins, assembled in Mistress Hopkins' big kitchen, learning from Hobomok's wife the craft of moccasin making; the soft foot-coverings were both comfortable and warm for the babies. But the lesson is interrupted and Hobomok takes his wife away, saying that the governor wants her. The surprise of the women is lessened only by apprehension when they later learn that she had been sent on a mission which none of

them could have performed, nor was a man of theirs
able to cope with its delicacy, not even Hobomok.
This peculiar circumstance was caused by Squanto,
their other trusted interpreter and friend. He had
stated that all was not well with their Indian allies
and that Massasoit was treacherously planning with
the Narragansetts to exterminate them. The quali-
fications of Hobomok's wife were at once apparent
to the men in consultation over this news, which
Hobomok insistently declared could not be true. She
was instructed, therefore, under guise of a casual
visitor, to go to Massasoit's camp and learn what
she could. Her return was anxiously awaited. She
accomplished her errand in a most satisfactory and
creditable manner, and her information relieved
them of alarm.

Another year passed, with a not very succesful
harvest; uncertain Indian affairs, and the arrival of
boats bringing letters, even visitors but no supplies
or friends or families — the Merchants and even
Robert Cushman seemed to fail them.

Some of the boats brought men whom they supported for a time from their scanty supply, who had
come out to establish another colony on the coast and
who requited their kindness by ingratitude and
scorn for a settlement having women. Another boat,
however, was more acceptable as proving they had
friends in need, though unknown, for by it word was
brought of a massacre of Virginia colonists by the
Indians. From this same kind-hearted ship captain,
John Huddleston, Edward Winslow — who visited

him to extend the colony's thanks for the warning —
was able to procure some provisions, of which they
were greatly in need, and thereby increased their
bread allowance to a quarter of a pound a day.
From this warning also they proceeded to build a
stronger and larger fort, one part being planned for
a place of worship.

A trading ship coming in, made them pay exorbi-
tantly for their needs seeing how greatly they lacked
them. On this ship, however, was a gentleman who
was returning to England from Virginia. He made
the acquaintance of the Plymouth people while the
ship was in the harbor, and that he was a welcome
visitor to the Brewster household is told by a letter
he later sent to Governor Bradford saying how he
had enjoyed Mr. Brewster's books. A man of like
tastes, evidently, and his passing acquaintance a
pleasant incident to them.

The autumn and winter were punctuated by trips
taken by the governor and some of the other men,
with Squanto, in search of camps where the Indians
would sell corn, as their own harvest was far from
being enough to keep them until the next. On one
of these expeditions, Squanto died.

As planting time approached, in view of the fact
that the next harvest must produce a much greater
amount, to avoid the dangers of starvation which
they were then enduring, the governor, in consultation, decided to divide the land into personal holdings, instead of all lands being worked for and held
by the community. This new plan quickly grew

increased enthusiasm for planting and culture, since
emulation and friendly contests for success began.
Mary Chilton and Humility Cooper were each given
an acre, and the attention those acres received was
not less than any other. To work in one's very own
soil was pleasure as well as profit, discounting the
fatigue.

At this time, also, the women had a particularly
choice bit of satisfaction. No less than the total
disestablishment and wreck of the colony which the
men had come to plant who had accepted hospitality
from the Plymouth people, when they arrived, and
so discourteously returned it by ridiculing a settlement which contained women. Appeals for help
from them were received, and with usual generosity
were granted, to enable them to keep their lives from
starvation and the Indians, and to leave that country.

Plymouth had but six matrons; and the young
woman who had been maid to Mrs. Carver, and four
young girls, Priscilla, Mary, Elizabeth and Humility,
with Remember Allerton and Constance Hopkins
fast leaving childhood in the responsibilities of this
difficult life. With so many single men the widow
and the girls could have a half dozen at command in
an instant, while Mary Brewster had four strong
right arms to rely on, her husband and three sons;
Susanna Winslow the hands of her husband, brother
and brothers-in-law, Gilbert and John, at need. Remember and Constance had each a brother to call
upon and the other two married women, husbands

and sons. Nevertheless, no one would care to deny that the twenty-four hours of the day of these loyal and efficient members of the company were not as heavily laden as those of the men, nor that their efforts in sustaining the struggling community were not as valuable in the final results.

"They made the home and kept the hearth fires
      burning;
They spun and wove and tilled the barren soil;
They met each day's return with patient trusting
And murmured not through all the weary toil."

THE BRIDE SHIP.

THE BRIDE SHIP.

Massasoit was ill — very ill, and a Dutch ship had run aground near his encampment. This news, brought by runners, caused Winslow to again leave his family and penetrate the forests to visit the Chief, as he was looked upon as a special friend of Massasoit, and could speak Dutch. It was about a year from the time when Hobomok's wife went over the trail on her diplomatic errand. The Dutch ship had gotten away, but Massasoit was decidedly ill. Among Winslow's talents was skill in doctoring and nursing, so with some remedies and food he had carried with him, he was able to improve the condition of the Chief. Massasoit's delight and gratitude manifested themselves in an important piece of information, which was that an Indian conspiracy was in the making against Plymouth. With this startling revelation Winslow returned. The matter was soon concluded, for their Captain, as he believed preparation and prevention were better than cure, took a picked company and the offensive, and came back with the head of the bold ringleader. This salutary but grewsome object caused the women to look elsewhere than the point on the battlements of the fort where it was displayed. However the warning had its effect — discontented Indians be-came mild in terror of the Sword of the White Men,

as they called Myles Standish. The picked company
in this event was composed of several of the young
men who were specially, if secretly, favored by Priscilla, Mary and Elizabeth.

Ships and more letters, one bringing truly joyful
news that, at last, some of their own people would
come in the next ships sent out by the Merchants.
This cheer was sorely needed, but as they were just
managing to keep from starvation by the fish as
almost their only food, they wondered how they
could supply the newcomers with a living. The
prospect was indeed dreary, as a protracted drought
had wilted their cherished crops hopelessly. Another ship, bringing a rather important naval official in
charge of fishing activities on the coast, came in.
This officer, Captain Francis West, called Admiral
of New England, made but a short stay, but long
enough to fill them with anxiety as he told them he
had spoken a ship at sea, had boarded her, found
her bound for this port, and sailed in company with
her until in a violent storm they lost sight of her.
He supposed she had already come in, and, finding
she had not, feared some mischance.

These summer days were dark for them, starving,
with hopes of a harvest blighted by drought, and
now distress for the possible loss of the ship bringing their loved ones. In this deepest gloom, which
proved the fore-runner of dawn, they set apart a
day of prayer, in humility and distress, by their
faith's steady flame. Under the glaring sun, the
day began — but at evening the sun set in clouds

and the rain came for which they prayed. The corn, the fruit was saved.

Sweet and soft was the air of the summer morning some few weeks after this; birds sang joyously and a silver mist hung over the sea as Plymouth awoke to the new day. The women seemed more light-hearted than of late, shown by snatches of song now and then as they pursued the common tasks of the household. An indefinable feeling which had come to them that since the answer to their prayer for rain had been given by many refreshing showers, the one in supplication for the safety of the ship and their expected dear ones could not be in vain and all would yet be well, gave them more enjoyment of life notwithstanding a breakfast of boiled clams was all they could prepare for their families. The smoke from the chimneys rose over the thatched roofs, pointing seaward. Some of the men came forth from their homes, on their way to the day's labors, and cheerily greeted one another, stopping to speak of the weather and prospects of plenty.

Mary Brewster stands in her door-way, arranging the sprays of the wild rose trained beside it — the showers had revived it and it looked its best. She had planted and tended it, hoping for the day when her daughters might smile at her beside its blossoms. Priscilla joins her in admiring it, both thinking of Fear and Patience on the longed for ship. They speak of this being the first ship to come having a woman's name, and that she was bringing so many women.

John Alden stops on his way past with a morning greeting. What man more anxious than he for the arrival of the *Anne*, though his bride-to-be is not on the ship. Through many months Priscilla has heard love's voice, sweet and low, tender and strong, and though for one reason and another it seemed best to wait, she has now promised to marry him when the uncertainty about the ship is over, for she could not leave dear Mistress Brewster, who had so mothered her, in the suspense concerning her own daughters, nor be selfish in thinking of her own affairs when the universal anxiety was so great.

They too, talk of the weather, of the breeze from the southwest, and glance at the chimney's long finger of smoke pointing, pointing to the sea. Half unconsciously they look in that direction and watch the thinning fog as it seems to form in patterns like Flemish lace, as Priscilla says. Now it has parted and the sun's brilliancy streams through making a jewelled pathway on the water. Quickly Priscilla grasps Mary Brewster's hand and flings out her arm in the direction the smoke has been pointing. Against the pink and golden morning sky there is a ship, coming slowly, slowly, into the harbor, flinging before her wreaths of pearly foam. The *Anne!*

"Then from their houses in haste came forth the
        Pilgrims of Plymouth,
Men and women and children all hurrying down to
        the sea shore."
Never again did the Pilgrims of Plymouth expe-

rience the thrill of that moment at the arrival of
any ship, and only once before had the feeling approached it — at the arrival of the *Fortune*. Though
some emotions were similar in each case, such as
relief and joy, the circumstances were dissimilar.
The relief was for themselves, for their own welfare, in the first case, in the second their relief was
doubled, as the welfare of those on the ship was the
chief thought. The first joy was coupled with surprise at its unexpectedness, the second with thanksgiving at the fulfillment of a great hope and antici-
pation.

Fathers and husbands, brothers and friends
jumped into boats to put off to the *Anne* to see and
greet at the earliest possible moment those of whom
they had been thinking and dreaming for so long.
Here is Richard Warren, Doctor Fuller and Francis
Cooke, of the first division, Jonathan Brewster and
Thomas Prence, of the second, off in the first dash.
The governor's boat takes also his assistant, Isaac
Allerton, and Captain Myles Standish. Those on
the ship, crowding along the rail, see the boats
coming to them over the laughing wavelets, and
recognizing one after another of the men as they
come alongside, laugh in reply as they wave.

There has been written some charming verses
descriptive of the arrival in this country of the
foreign girls who married members of the A. E. F.
of the recent war. The conclusion fits well with
that scene of nearly three hundred years ago :

"They loved our heroes well enough
    To leave all else besides
And make America their own,
    So welcome home the brides."

Yes, and wives, too. The ship's band, if there had
been one, might well have played the tune of
"Sweethearts and Wives," while Plymouth's drum
and fife could have replied with "Haste to the
Wedding," or "Here Comes the Bride."

When the excitement had subsided a little, in a
few days time, the Brewster girls had the interesting
event of a wedding in their home, for their old
friend, Priscilla married the young man of her
choice, whom they had never seen, until they came
to Plymouth. There was little wherewith to make a
wedding feast, but, at least a health could be given
the bride and bridegroom in the elderblow wine,
made a year before.

Indeed the great shock to the newcomers was the
condition of affairs in the colony — the thinness,
paleness and weakness of all, from want of sufficient
food. The governor recalls for many a day the embarrassment felt by the Pilgrims that so little could
be offered to the new arrivals, only fish and cold
water. But the *Anne,* unlike the *Fortune,* brought
some supplies and necessaries, so the passengers were
not a drain upon the colony as in the case of the
Fortune, but, rather a great help.

Following the example of John Alden, Francis
Eaton took to himself a wife, thereby adding another
to the number of married women among the original
company. He wedded the only woman who has been

without a name in the history of the *Mayflower* and
of the colony, perhaps the only woman in history
who, being mentioned several times, has always been
nameless. Of course she had a name and was called
by it by her contemporaries, but seek as we may,
she is designated only for us as "Mrs Carver's
maid." For Francis Eaton she stayed, when she
might have returned with Desire Minter; for him
and his baby boy, left motherless, in the first winter,
who had been looked after by plain but kind-hearted
Eleanor Billington.

A passenger by the *Anne* whom we know, the
wealthy widow, Mrs. Alice Southworth, brought her
maid — but she was Christian Penn, and she married Francis Eaton for his third wife in after years,
as the second Mrs. Eaton (we are glad to give her a
name for once), did not live long.

The *Anne* stayed at Plymouth over a month — a
witness of the several marriages which she had
brought about, directly and indirectly.

Alice Carpenter — the lovely English girl, going
with her family into voluntary exile in Leyden,
marrying there and afterwards living, a prosperous
matron of London, as Alice Southworth, then cross-
ing the sea, a widow, to become a bride again, this
time of a Colonial governor, living thereafter as
Alice Bradford, an adornment of the community
about her and a great factor in its peace and progress — weaves one of the bright threads of romance
through the story of the women of Plymouth. The
governor's marriage to the charming widow was

indeed an important event in the life of the village.

Somewhat of a surprise to all but a few, was the announcement of the coming marriage of the Captain to an old friend, who had come out in company with Mrs. Southworth, for the same reason, in answer to a proposal of marriage, by letter. Then followed another wedding, of special interest to all the first comers by the *Mayflower* and to many of the recent arrivals, that of big John Howland with little Elizabeth Tilly, as she always seemed to her old friends, though quite grown up now and nearing seventeen. John Howland had patiently waited, as other men. Thus, by the coming of the *Anne,* bringing her own dear daughters, after three years of separation, Mary Brewster was able to smile at the departure of two of her loving daughters of adversity, to homes of their own. In this practical and primitive life, no honeymoons could be thought of. Plymouth, itself, then lay within the radius of a quarter of a mile and there was not another civilized habitation in hundreds of leagues, so the only wedding journey of these *Mayflower* girls, Priscilla and Elizabeth, was from Elder Brewster's doorway to their own new homes; one down, one up the street. We know that these girls had in addition to the loving interest of Mary Brewster, the affectionate encouragement of Susanna Winslow and the warm friendship of their girl companions of Leyden and of Plymouth, Fear and Patience Brewster, Mary Chilton and Humility Cooper — priceless wedding gifts — nor lacking was the regard of the governor's

wife, a contemporary bride and old friend of Leyden days.

Of these marriages we have not a sketch in the
written history of those days, except in the new
book brought by the *Anne* for the colony's records,
and the first entries, most appropriately, are these.
And that the *Fortune* might be represented in the
weddings of this season, as well as the *Mayflower*
an *Anne,* the widow, Mrs. Ford, proceeded to take
a second husband, in the person of Peter Brown,
one of the sturdy and loyal men of the colony, who
had come in the *Mayflower.*

The doctor's young wife, Bridget; Richard Warren's daughters, as well as their mother, and Hester
Cooke and Juliana Morton, all arrivals by the *Anne,*
hardly realized at first the sombre background
of the life against which these marriages shone out
for the first comers. To them it seemed they had
arrived in a land of weddings and happiness —
though lack of feasting and trousseaux was somewhat
evident. Another interested on-looker, is the aunt
of Remember and Mary, Isaac Allerton's sister,
whom we knew in Leyden as Sarah Priest, but,
widowed the first winter after her husband arrived
at the new home he was to prepare for her, she
nevertheless came to Plymouth with a new husband, whom she had recenly married in Leyden, and
now she is Sarah Cuthbertson. She brought the little
sister of the Allerton children, Sarah, who had been
left in her care, but did not give up charge of her.

The augmented motion and sounds on Plymouth's

street, under the September sky was apparent.
Many women had come; numerous children were
there; the men's families were forming new households; strangers getting accustomed to one another
and surroundings; friends renewing old ties — the
newcomers feeling a bit lost, nevertheless.

The life, such as it had been, for the *Mayflower*
passengers was over. That time, within the three
years from their departure on the *Speedwell* from
Delfshaven, to their welcome of the *Anne*, at Plymouth, was a thing apart.

BENEATH THE PINES OF PLYMOUTH.

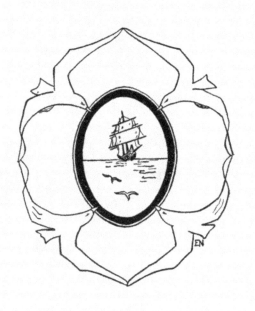

BENEATH THE PINES OF PLYMOUTH.

The *Anne*, laden with lumber, furs and mail, sailed in September, carrying also an important passenger; Susanna Winslow had to spare her husband for a time, while he went to England on the colony's business and his own affairs. However, her cares now were somewhat lessened by the coming in the *Anne* of a young women, named Mary Becket, to assist in her household labors. Since his other aunt had come, by the *Anne*, to live in Plymouth, little Samuel Fuller went back to the doctor's house to grow up. Bridget Fuller came with the baby, who was too delicate to make the voyage in the *Mayflower*, now three years old, and the doctor's sunny gentle spirit rejoiced.

Following the *Anne* came a small ship called *Little James*, which was to remain for the colony's use. It proved of little use and great expense, after all, but it brought other Leyden friends, as well as strangers from England. Thus Plymouth grew, and this autumn saw about a hundred and eighty persons instead of the handful who had struggled for life and a home in the wilderness for the past three years.

The new plan of individual division of the land with its planting and care proved its wisdom; the crops ripening rapidly, foretold an abundant harvest; the lightening of hearts and the promising outlook caused the governor to proclaim a day of public thanksgiving. It was not after the manner of that of two years previously, as conditions were different, but more in remembrance of the day of supplication held in July. The dreaded visitor famine, was gone, never to return to the firesides of Plymouth — although for some awful hours it seemed possible. On a wintry night, too great a fire on the hearth of one of the new houses, caused that house, and those nearest, to be consumed by flames and to threaten the Common House where their trading supplies and harvest were stored. Well that the Captain had prepared his original company to fight possible fire as well as possible hostile attack, for by those men was that tragedy averted, as, in the excitement and confusion, the majority of the new-comers were more of a hindrance than help. The women must have felt that if cares and labors were somewhat decreased, responsibility and uncertainty were increased through the added numbers to the town.

That winter was the gayest Plymouth had ever known. Families had been so lately reunited that the satisfaction and joy of the occasion still caused effervescence of spirits, and, too, there were many more young people who never had to live through the hard and perilous times which the first group experienced. These all had either homes to go to or loving friends to shelter them until homes were built; no sickness to contend with and plenty to eat.

Where the comforts of all the men had depended more or less on a few women, now the hands of many women made all tasks lighter, and there was time for more social intercourse, which though in simplest form was sufficient then for relaxation and pleasure. No wonder happy voices were carried on the winter winds and light footsteps echoed on the street. Neighborliness being ever a characteristic of the Pilgrims, there was a constant exchange of goodwill and kindly attentions between the households. They had not needed Robert Cushman's admonition in his discourse to them, before returning in the *Fortune,* "There is no grief so tedious as a churlish companion and nothing makes sorrows easy more than cheerful associates. Bear ye therefore one another's burdens and be not a burden one to another," but they did not ignore it.

We may glance in the houses, on a frosty evening, and see who are sheltered within their cosy brightness and warmth. The governor's house has a large and merry party to hold, for he and his wife are entertaining for the winter, her sister, Juliana, with husband, George Morton and all the little Mortons: Patience, Nathaniel, John, Sarah, Ephraim and baby George; also a regular member of the family, Thomas Cushman. No wonder Christian Penn was in demand.

In the Brewster home, across the way, the Elder and his wife have also lively company, with three sons, the dear daughters, and Mary Chilton and Humility Cooper and Richard More. Thomas

Prence, John Winslow, Philip de la Noye and half
a dozen more of the young men drop in of an evening, with four attractive girls and charming hostess
to welcome them, and even an older man occasionally, as when Isaac Allerton brings his daughter over
to join in the fun; though he appears only to talk
to the Elder he glances at one of the girls, sometimes. Patience has her little flax wheel at one side
of the room under a candle bracket and the whir
of the wheel makes a background for the voices.
Thomas Prence is beside her mightily interested in
the spinning, as the product is for his sweetheart's
hope chest. The Brewster girls have brought a
supply of new linens to their mother, from Holland,
and indeed all the housekeepers are well supplied
with this necessity, but constant usage wears out
the best made and so more must be in readiness,
therefore spinning is a regular occupation, especially
for those with a wedding in mind.

Susanna Winslow has company, also, this evening, for her brother, the cheerful doctor, and his
young wife have been having supper with her and
her young brothers-in-law. John has gone over to
the Brewster's, but Gilbert, his handsome, rather
discontented face lit by the fire, sits near the hearth,
smoking, with the doctor and another man, for
Sarah Cuthbertson has come in for an evening's
gossip with her old friend, Anna, bringing her new
husband. The three women have much to talk of —
matters both grave and gay — and the new-comers
from Leyden are doing most of the chatter, Susanna

well pleased to listen, commenting occasionally on the narration of who had married or moved away and such items of interest as would accumulate in three years, with infrequent opportunities of communication.

John Howland and his Elizabeth go in the doorway of the Alden's house for a social call — and find Francis Cooke and his wife, Hester, there, also, and soon after, the Captain and his wife, Barbara, enter, and there is laughter and chat, while the women's fingers ply the knitting needles, for even in recreation moments the women can seldom afford to be wholly idle. Hester is an old Leyden friend to Priscilla and Elizabeth, though not of English birth, while Barbara is a new friend to them all, Hester having made her acquaintance on the sea voyage which brought them both to Plymouth. Francis Cooke had a comfortable house awaiting his wife and children, and Hester, naturally, quite fitted in with the first comers.

In the large house of the Hopkins, we see a number of the youngest inhabitants of Plymouth having a very jolly time — Giles and Constance being responsible. Here are Mary and Bartholomew Allerton, John and Jane Cooke, Patience Morton and Thomas Cushman, Ann and Sarah Warren, William Palmer and Samuel Jenny, even Jacob Cooke and Damaris Hopkins are admitted, also Mercy Sprague, Samuel Fuller, Resolved White and Sarah Annable, for at these children's parties the early hours kept could not rob even the youngest of much sleep. We

know how many of the future marriages in Plymouth came from this gay group. Stephen Hopkins
and his wife have gone out themselves and we see
them in the home of Richard Warren, whose wife
and daughter Mary, having gotten the youngest
girls, Elizabeth and Abigail, in bed are glad to welcome company. Two of their fellow passengers in
the *Anne* are also present, one being Robert Bartlett,
whose interest in Mary began on their ocean voyage,
which has a very modern sound. The other visitor
is Ellen Newton, who came out with these friends,
and is soon to marry John Adams, who preceded her
in the *Fortune.*

Here is another gathering at the home of John
and Sarah Jenny, who, with their three children,
arrived on the *Little James,* they are of the old Leyden company; also we see here Stephen Tracy and
Triphosa, his French wife and their little girl,
Sarah, who has come to have a frolic with her playmates, Abigail and Sarah, while the parents are ab-
sorbed in their own affairs; they are soon joined
by William Palmer (who came with his son in the
Fortune) and his wife, Frances, a passenger in the
Anne. The happy-go-lucky, or unlucky, household
of the Billingtons is evidently satisfied with its own
family this evening.

And to look further we see other homes whose
inmates are strangers to us, though not to all of
our earlist acquaintances, such as Francis and Anna
Sprague, whose little girl, Mercy, is at the Hopkins,
this evening; Anthony and Jane Annable, their

oldest child we have also seen at the party but Sarah and Hannah are at home; Ralph Wallen and Joyce, his wife, Edward and Rebecca Bangs, with two children romping at home; Robert Hicks with Margaret and three children; also Mr. and Mrs. Edward Burcher, Mr. and Mrs. Thomas Flavell and Mr. and Mrs. William Hilton and little boys (all of the latter arrived by the *Anne*) besides numerous single men of the *Fortune, Anne* and *Little James,* who are quite welcome at the different houses. With so many young men, the girls had numbers to choose from, as each would have been glad for a wife and home of his own. Light refreshments add to the social hour we see, possets and manchets with home-brewed ale, and nuts, or the beverage made of roots, flavored with sassafras, similar to modern root beer, and popcorn — both the latter Indian additions to their knowledge. The possets and manchets are little cakes, the former sometimes called "sweet shrub" made of flour, sugar and spice, while manchets are flour, made without the spice and baked brown like our cookies.

Having thus seen who is who in Plymouth by the lights of the houses, "shining like stars in the dark and mist of the evening," we will observe some passing events, from this time, which were of interest to the women, either for themselves or members of their families or friends.

This happy winter passed into their history, and spring coming found the Plymouth people with hearts more in tune to the joy and hope of its opening buds and bird songs than ever before.

On a March day, the first ship of the season from England came into view. If one has ever lived, in modern times, far from native land and many dear friends, as on island possessions, for instance, in civil or military life, with ships coming safely to harbor, the only chance of communication with the outside world, bringing letters, packages of gifts or a friend or two, perchance, with weeks or months of interval between sight of a ship from overseas, one may easily comprehend just how the women of Plymouth felt when a ship was coming in. And though the women did not write or receive letters very often, in those days, yet they heard the contents of those which frequently came to their husbands and could think and talk of the tidings for many a day.

The *Charity* brought Susanna Winslow's husband home to her and to his welcoming friends. His mission had been eminently successful and proved the adage of "If you want a thing done well, do it yourself," for Winslow knowing each need of the colony, brought back the proper supplies for trade with the Indians or the fishing ships, and adequate selection of clothing for all. Having a wife, he knew what to buy for the women, and what the children needed, besides special commissions in way of books or household comforts as they existed, at that time, elsewhere. The colony was not rich — either as a whole or by individual wealth — but though bearing a heavy debt to the Merchants, they had to live

while every effort was being made to reduce the
original, and the Merchants were usually willing to
add to their obligation, especially since their exports were so marketable. Also some of the families
had personal credit in England, even though for
several years the results of their trade went to reduce the common debt, and the only personal gain
allowed in Plymouth was from selling the products
of their own lands to one another. Corn was legal
tender, nothing else was needed or of greater value
to them or the natives, until a later date. Therefore
the Elder, the Governor, the Captain, could rejoice
in more books, the women in the last word of costume
detail from London or Leyden suitable to their
present situation. We are quite sure that Mary
Chilton, Patience Brewster and the other girls, as
well as the young brides, were just as particular
about the set of a broad brimmed hat, or the ribbons
on a velvet hood, as interested in whether white neck-
wear had bows or tassels to fasten it, and if silver
shoe buckles were engraved or plain, as any woman
of today in her up-to-date appearance.

In addition to the many personal interests connected with Edward Winslow's return, he had purchased several head of cattle, and the children
watched with greatest curiosity — and some alarm
to those who had never seen such creatures — the
approach of the small boats from the ship with ropes
trailing behind attached to the horns and necks of
the cows, swimming valiantly to their new home.
Their familiar appearance brought an increased

home feeling to the women. From that day milk
was never lacking for beverage, butter, and cheese;
goat's milk was no longer their only supply.

And of great interest to many was a certain book
which Winslow had written and had printed that
winter, in London, called "Good News From New
England." This publication which threw the picture of themselves and their surroundings sharply
before the eyes of many on the screen of public intelligence, in England, was a factor in their life
thereafter by its results. Business for the colony
was not concluded at the time Winslow wished to
return to Plymouth, and, as he brought letters re-
questing his further presence, to continue these
matters, the governor agreed to his leaving them
again, and Susanna could do nothing but consent
also.

The *Charity* remained for fishing, throughout the
summer, which was crowded with events of moment.
In response to appeals from the Pilgrims in Plymouth to the Merchants in London that their pastor,
John Robinson, be sent to them with others of their
number from Leyden, the Merchants had made ex-
cuses. The *Anne* brought affectionate letters from
Robinson but not his longed-for presence. To their
great surprise, therefore, in company with Winslow,
on the *Charity*, there came a stranger whom the Merchants had decided should be the colony's religious
head. In vain had Winslow argued and pleaded for
Robinson, knowing what a disappointment this
would be. This minister brought his wife and

children and at first seemed well disposed toward
the Pilgrims, so they accepted what they could not
help and allowed him a seat on the Council board —
for now there were several assistants to the governor
— and requested him to act as associate with their
elder, but although he declared himself a convert to
the Separatist church, they did not admit him to the
position of their pastor. A more acceptable companion on this home-coming of Winslow's was a
clever and likable young carpenter, who did them
good service.

In the early summer, Ellen Newton married John
Adams, which was of interest to those who had
crossed with her in the *Anne*, and kindly observed
by others. In midsummer, two new comers brought
rejoicing and pleasure to many. In the governor's
family arrived the baby who received the name of
William, which had also been given to his father,
grand-father and great-grandfather. Into John and
Priscilla Alden's home came Elizabeth, called the
first born daughter of the Pilgrims. As one writer
has expressed it, ''She was destined to outlive every
individual then in the colony and to survive the
colony itself by twenty-five years.''

In August, just about a year from the time of the
arrival of the *Anne*, another of her passengers became a bride, making the eighth in the colony during
the twelve-month. This wedding was of special interest, not only because it was the first in a prominent family, but because of the popularity of the
bride and the groom and the affection and esteem

in which the parents were held. Plymouth rejoiced
when Patience Brewster married Thomas Prence,
and her mother felt that she then had all that heart
could wish for. With tall, affectionate sons and loving daughters, one going to a home of her own, but
not away, and, beside her, the handsome lover of her
youth as her devoted husband, sharing her feelings
on this important day; a home with all comforts
then obtainable; among admiring friends as of old,
Mary Brewster sighed in happy content. Plymouth
had returned to her the pleasures of Scrooby without its later uncertainties and trials. And Patience,
a reflection of her mother's early fairness and charm,
was as radiant a bride as New England's sun ever
lighted on a wedding day. Her young husband was
to steadily advance in the esteem of the colony and
in material position, reaching the important place of
governor in a few years. Thus destiny had woven
for her life a beautiful pattern, with childhood in
Scrooby, girlhood in Leyden, womanhood in Plymouth, with love and tender care to lighten all her
days. A bright particular star in the galaxy of
women of Plymouth colony who were not of the *Mayflower* company, but who found their life's fulfillment there.

Plymouth society had grown enough to be no
longer the one and indivisible association welded together by common experiences and mutual interests,
as it was at first. With the advent of those uncon-
nected with the original pioneers and their objects,

who came as friends of the Merchants or as adventurers to a new but firmly established country, caring nothing for its interests, rather hoping to throw over what the first comers had won by their courage and faith (of firm government and laws, freedom of conscience and liberality for those of differing views, and united labor for prosperity and peace) came a change; a division was felt between the group with the anarchist spirit and that comprising the original element. Regretting this, but forced to acknowledge it by definite unpleasantness between them, the first families began to live within their own circle as much as possible. Stirring scenes took place, as autumn began, and the women had much to discuss. The governor was forced to make the issue and in upholding law and order to dismiss certain members of the community, though their families were allowed to stay and were cared for until new homes could be procured elsewhere. Chief among these disturbers of Plymouth's peace were a group who had come in the *Anne,* under leadership of one, John Oldham, and the hypocritical minister, Lyford, who was a sad disappointment to these charitably inclined people. The recital of this experience has been given in many of the writings which concern the men of Plymouth — the "Pilgrim Fathers," so often mentioned. The element of unrest being removed, other persons, not harmful but formerly indifferent only, became loyal supporters of the commonwealth; so calmness again settled over Plymouth when the first snow flakes draped the

rugged pines, standing as sentinels or guardians for
this little world, between the wilderness and the sea.

The winter was much like the one preceding it,
with two new young housekeepers and the prospect
of other brides. Susanna Winslow was again without her husband, and Gilbert had decided to revisit
his old home — accompanying his brother to England, never to return. Matchmakers would gladly
have mated him with one of the colony's belles. One
wonders, even at this distant day, why this eligible
young bachelor did not marry, what woman touched
his heart? Pity he had not asked Desire to stay;
perhaps it was she that was the something Plymouth
lacked for him; or did he admire Mary Chilton's
graces of mind and person, yet leave her for his
brother John's happiness? Fancies play around a
possible answer to this passing question among the
many love stories that we know in Plymouth, which
culminated for the principals, as fairy tales, in subsequent happiness.

Grey days and golden passed over Plymouth,
each one finding the women busy with the successive
round of household duties and industries, not ended
with the sunset gun as the men's labors might be.
Let us look at a list of occupations which kept them
from idleness in each season of the year: candle-
making, pickling eggs, preserve and cordial making,
distilling of herbs, ale or beer making, manufacture
of soap, laundrying, dying cloths and yarns, braid-
ing mats of rushes, sweeping and sanding floors,
cleaning wooden and iron utensils, scouring and

polishing pewter, brass and silver articles, pounding
corn, butter and cheese making, cooking, weaving,
spinning, sewing, drying wet shoes by placing hot
oats in them, or clothes — storm soaked — by blazing logs on the hearth (for umbrellas and overshoes
were then unknown) and teaching the boys and
girls. It was not until a later day that there were
schools for the children, and as it had been in England, so in their new home, their learning was obtained from their elders. Some had brought what
books they could; nearly all brought Bibles in several languages, Psalm-books and Catechisms, and
before long, the almanacs proved a most useful
factor in home education.

Moments of recreation and rest were evidently
somewhat rare, but no less enjoyable, lighter occupations serving the purpose at home or when visiting. Can we not see them on many a winter evening
by the firelight of blazing cedar logs and candle glow
from the dips made in the autumn, with the fine em-
broidery and knitting in which the women of their
day and training took such pride; or placing the
stitches in the samplers which were to take the place
of pictures on the bare walls, also making designs
in colored threads upon the sets of curtains for
beds or windows; meanwhile talking together of past
days in their old homes — of the friends left there
whom they were hopefully expecting to join them,
showing keepsakes and telling their personal value
to amuse one another.

Doubtless their greatest peace and pleasure came

from singing songs as they had done in Pastor Robinson's house, looking out on the beautiful old garden in Leyden. The book from which they sang has been described in the poem we all know:
"The well-worn psalm book of Ainsworth
  Printed in Amsterdam, the words and music together,
  Rough-hewn, angular notes, like stones in the wall of a church-yard
  Darkened and overhung by the running vine of the verses.''
  Such was the book, the delight of the Pilgrim women, for in that country of few books, not only did its pages afford their only music, but the annotations formed both a dictionary and encyclopedia of useful knowledge; things temporal and things spiritual were explained, scientific, historical and religious information was dispensed therein. Truly a library in a single volume.
  Spring again, and the day of Edward Winslow's return found the town in excitement and the women decidedly disturbed. John Oldham had come suddenly amongst them, for no other purpose than to revile and insult the authorities. They had imprisoned him and were later getting rid of him in a chastened mood, when Winslow and the captain of the ship, which had brought him unnoticed into the harbor, walked up the street. John Oldham surprised them yet again, at a later day, but then returned to make amends and apologies, and to offer services, which the authorities were able to accept. And this man, with the upsetting propensities, met

a violent death at the hands of Indians in Massachusetts bay — his boat was rescued and his death
avenged by Captain John Gallup, Senior, of Boston.
This event has been called the first naval engagement
of American history, and in it were the seeds of the
Pequot war.

As John Oldham's boat put out from the harbor,
and the boats from the *Jacob* landed the colony's
supplies and Winslow's belongings, the unpleasantness was soon forgotten in welcoming him and the
popular captain, William Pierce, now an old friend,
by his frequent visits to Plymouth with various
ships. One special parcel Edward Winslow delivered with care to the governor's wife. It was a
gift to her of a package of spices from her old friend,
Robert Cushman, in London.

The bountiful summer was enjoyed in "peace and
health and contented minds." We may think of the
women in their gardens tending lovingly the plants
grown from seeds carefully brought from other
gardens, far away, where memories must have been
tended as well as flowers. Those who would, might
join the children and dogs in walks on the sea
shore and in the woods, bringing to their homes
decorations in the form of flowers and shells. One
writer has said, "The first ornaments of the houses
were probably the periwinkle shells, their memory
deserves to be cherished like the arbutus flower
among the things that awaken Pilgrim memories."

The first quickly built dwellings were now solidi-
fied into comfortable houses, various rooms being

added from time to time, with furniture colony-made
or imported; the ground plots around them were
kept attractively, some of them being washed by the
bubbling waters of Town Brook, as it flowed past,
and most of them enclosed with palings or wooden
walls, against which fruit trees and vines were
trained, as in kitchen gardens of the old country.
Sometimes at day's close, it was possible to watch or
partake in the old English game of stool-ball, a
distant cousin of croquet.

An evening in late summer beautifies the land-
scape with its serene light. Through the garden behind the house, Mary Brewster walks with her
daughters. They come toward the brook and pause
to enjoy their surroundings. From the woodland
across the stream the purple and golden flowers
of the season bend toward them in the lightest of
airs; the robins fly from bush to tree, preparing to
rest. We seem to feel with them the remembrance
of another scene of a summer evening long passed,
when these three walked down through the grounds
of Scrooby Manor to Ryton Stream to say farewell.
But Town Brook does not see the same expression
of sadness and uncertainty among them as Ryton
saw; the long shafts of illuminating light reveal
countenances where only satisfaction and tranquility
dwell.

The kitchen at the Winslow's presents a lively
scene this autumn morning. The Mistress and Mary
Becket are in the depths of preparations for a feast

and not an ordinary one. Susanna is registering great cheerfulness and Mary decided efficiency. Two important causes may be found both for the feast and good spirits. First, the master of the house returned yesterday from a somewhat hazardous but extremely successful trading trip far up the coast. The principal men of the old set were with him, so several other wives were also rejoicing at the return. The great quantity of beaver would make who would, a fur coat for the coming winter, like those the Indian women wore so comfortably. And as for Mary — why George Soule had told her last evening that she was the only woman for him, and indeed she would not be as long making up her mind on that subject as Mary Chilton had been in making up hers on a like matter. All of which shows that an elaborate cooking program was a small matter this morning. And the feast? Why, it is to be a supper party in compliment to Mary Chilton and John Winslow who have recently become engaged. The date hinged on Edward Winslow's return, but it had been thoroughly planned when he left. George Soule had been shooting one day and brought home a number of plump birds and a pair of wild turkeys.

These two are not the sole occupants of the kitchen, for others come and go. George Soule keeps up the noble fire by adding great oak sticks to the andirons in the mammoth fire-place and adjusting the multitude of hooks and chains and cooking utensils as they are needed. From the crane, big iron kettles exhale delicious odors, while numerous

skillets hold different important positions, the contents of each cooking at its appointed degree of heat,
while on the high mantle shelf above, the hour glass
is watched and turned. As the great oven door is
opened, what fragrance! Simmels, buns, biscuits
and pastry and what besides! Enter an Indian
with a bag of oysters specially ordered, since none
are in Plymouth waters; they are to be baked in
individual scallop shells, in the old, yet familiar way,
with breadcrumbs and butter. Mrs. Hopkins comes
with the kindly object of showing just how she
manufactures on rare occasions her wonderful dish
called "Hennes in Brette." The hens must be
scalded and cut in pieces, fried lightly with pork,
spice and crumbs, basted with ale, and colored gold
with saffron. The turkeys are stuffed with beechnuts
and will be roasted on the spit. A plum pudding is
bubbling in one of the kettles, and dumplings of flour
in another, to garnish the chicken dish; pumpkin
pies are made and standing aside, so too, loaves of
brown and white bread. Vegetables await their turn
— samp, onions, parsnips, turnips, peas; the succo-
tash is mixed, composed of corn, beans and meat. A
ham is boiling, likewise clam chowder. Mary pulls
a pan out of the oven — the nokake is done to a
turn!

Edward and John Winslow have thoughtfully
been asked for dinner by Mrs. Bradford — there
could hardly be much chance for them at home, this
day. Afternoon comes on apace and there is much
for the last part for Susanna and the last moments

for Mary and Hobomok's wife, who will help in the evening. The leg of mutton, rarest treat, with cucumber sauce, or couch, for the mutton to rest on is certainly perfection; the cucumbers, sliced and parboiled have drained, then butter fried, now, with condiments, onion, mutton gravy and lemon juice they are simmering gently, occasionally tossed about. A poloc, or stew of small birds, smothered with rice, onion and herbs, adds another to the wonderful combination of fragrance. And now come the partridges — a broth of boiled marrow bones, strained and put in an earthen dish with wine and spices is the delectable fluid in which they are cooked, the birds having been stuffed with whole peppers and marrow. Salad, cranberry tarts, grape jelly, pudding with strawberry sauce, and a marvelous sufflet, rich, frothing and crisp, (a pound roll of butter enlarged to half a dozen times its original size, from being turned on a long rod resting on the fire hooks, continuously dredged with flour and eaten as soon as possible.) Late in the day, Mrs. Warren comes in to direct the making of her special dish, another of the rarities, called cheese cake; boiled milk with beaten eggs has been cooling and curdling since last evening, it is now strained and to it added butter, mace, rose-water and wine, currants and syrup. Pastry forms are waiting to hold this combination for a few seconds in the oven. Elderblow wine (made by the old French receipt the women had learned on the Continent, of sugar, fruit, blossoms and yeast), cider, spiced ale and some of the excel-

lent wine which Edward Winslow brought on his
return from England, are to help digest this marvelous menu — and of great interest are the first ap-
ples from the Winslow's new orchard, likewise honey
from Plymouth bees, a recent industry.

Truly a feast—yet when it was ready, Susanna
met her guests with smiles, and renewed the admiration in the heart of her prospective young sister-in-
law. Those who partook of this supper and lived to
tell the tale were the old friends, of course, for Mary
Chilton was ever a favorite and one of the *Mayflower*
girls, so none of that list could be omitted, (Captain Standish on a mission in England, was missed),
and now that there was so large a younger set coming on to take the place of those who had married,
many of them must be invited, besides the recent
brides and bridegrooms, themselves, and one or two
of John Winslow's joyous and special friends of the
Fortune who might still be fancy free, but could not
be omitted on that account. That this invigorating
occasion was a success there is no doubt, and marked
a crest of the life of those first five years of the
Pilgrims in Plymouth.

Days go on, no matter how bright, they may not
be held. In a few years, changes — as ever.

We may look at a scene on another crisp autumn
morning. It is Sunday and there is stillness in the
town. Suddenly the drum rolls and people come
from their houses to assemble for the morning worship in the fort. The guard has formed in front of

the house of Captain Standish. Led by a sergeant, in rows of three abreast, followed by the Governor, the Elder, and the Captain, all wearing cloaks and carrying arms, they march silently up the hill. The rest of the population who may be going to the service this morning are ready to proceed also, for, unlike the severity of the rule from which these people fled, church attendance was expected but not compulsory. There are extra colors and numbers this morning. The town is entertaining a distinguished guest whose visit is to mark that tide in their affairs which, owing to their readiness to take at the flood, is to lead them on to fortune. Plymouth frequently entertains strangers, but this rotund, handsomely dressed gentleman, with the sharp eyes seeing all about him, with his several retainers and trumpeters, who walk on each side of him, though no notes are sounded this morning, is of more importance than any whom Plymouth has received. He represents the first foreign mission for commercial and personal benefits, and is the Secretary of the Dutch colony, five hundred miles to the southward, Isaac de Rasieres.

The intercourse already satisfactorily begun by negotiations culminating in this visit, was to be of mutual benefit for many years. The boat from Manhattan became a regularly welcomed bearer to Plymouth women of bright materials for clothes, sugar and other necessaries — in time quite the rival of a boat from England — the payment for these was by home grown tobacco, therefore nearly

as interesting a crop as corn. Even the latter was to
be replaced by something else as a medium of exchange through the visit of Monsieur de Rasieres.
Wampum, familiar word to us, but strange to Plymouth people, was to make an important and permanent appearance, and to prove that shells on the
shore were as a gold mine at the feet of the Pilgrims.

The ceremonious assent to the fort is accomplished, the congregation taking their places — the
women on one side of the room, the men on the
other, according to custom. To the visitor all is
strange, new and interesting. We rejoice in the days
he spent in Plymouth, for the advantage which came
to the Pilgrims and for the legacy which came to us
in the form of his written accounts of his visit.

As William Davidson, experienced statesman and
courtier, in a long ago visit to Scrooby, opened a
door of destiny through which it was appointed that
William Brewster was to lead this people into a new
world of liberty, so by this visit of Isaac de Rasieres,
travelled man of the world, to Plymouth, another
way was opened by which they were to reach, also
prosperity and prominence. The portraits of these
two men should hang as companion medallions in the
hall of Pilgrim memory, as doubtless they did in the
mind of William Brewster, himself having as much
worldly experience as either, with the personal attractions of each; loved friend of one, respected
acquaintance of the other.

At this time, the rather difficult role of step-mother was being played in three of the households. We know the families quite well, and are particularly interested in the women. The eldest in the position is Elizabeth Hopkins. If the part did not come easily to Stephen Hopkins' second wife, the responsibilities of it are now lessened, since Constance has recently added to the list of *Mayflower* brides by marrying Nicholas Snow and going to a home of her own. An impression seemed to prevail that Mistress Hopkins was rather jealous of her predecessor's son, Giles, on account of her own son, Caleb, yet it is through Giles only, that the name has been carried down to the present. Her four girls, Damaris, Deborah, Ruth and Elizabeth, made a lively home for any brother. Oceanus, born on the *Mayflower,* did not live beyond babyhood. The women of that day were just as human as of this, and amid all her fine qualities, if there was a little flaw, it no doubt came of her very fondness for her husband.

Across the street, in the governor's house, Alice Bradford has three boys to share the love and interest with her own, and the devotion of four. We have already seen one of them, Thomas Cushman, left by his father with Governor Bradford, until he should return to live in Plymouth — but Myles Standish, returning from his mission to England, had brought with other regretful tidings, the knowledge that Robert Cushman would not come again. Another fatherless boy, whom we have had but a glimpse of, is Nathaniel Morton, nephew to Alice Bradford.

George Morton lived but a short time as resident of
Plymouth, leaving his wife and family alone in the
new house, but the governor took Nathaniel to bring
up as a son, and Juliana Carpenter Morton married
again. The third boy is also fatherless in actual
sense; he has recently come to Plymouth, but to the
most loving mother and affectionate step-father boy
could desire, for this is Constant Southworth come
from London to his new home in the governor's
house in Plymouth, as his mother had done, whom
he strongly resembles in looks. And the fourth boy?
He is not fatherless, but has only lately come to renew both the acquaintance and affection of his pa-
rent, being John Bradford, from Amsterdam, youngest of the quartette, and seeing him we are reminded
of his girl mother, the governor's first wife. This
group is soon to be added to by Thomas Southworth,
whom his mother is expecting from England. We
can imagine these boys having a pretty good time
in the loving home of the Bradfords, and among
them grew up the three babies, half brothers and
half sister to John Bradford and the Southworth
boys — only one girl to amuse and tease them
through the years of childhood, the governor's
daughter, Mercy. Although step-mother to but one,
the part had no chance for prominence with Alice
Bradford, in being at the same time aunt to one,
friend to another and mother to five. Perhaps it
was because of this masculine element at home, that
Mistress Bradford was known for her special interest in the young girls of the colony — daughters of

her neighbors and playmates of her Mercy, such advantages and accomplishments as she had, she taught them. No wonder she welcomed her husband's suggestion of having her youngest sister, Priscilla Carpenter, come from England to make her home with them.

Another woman, of the style and character of Alice Bradford, the third and youngest step-mother, making such a success in her position as to prove her the good angel of the family into which she came, is Fear Brewster — now Mrs. Isaac Allerton. She already had the love of Bartholomew, Remember and Mary — quite grown out of childhood, but they must have been as surprised as the rest of the society of Plymouth that their father could win her for his wife, as he was so much older than she and always seeming rather preoccupied and self-satisfied. It speaks well for him that such was the case and that her attachment and loyalty never wavered through the brief years of her married life — and that it was a shield to him from public criticism or censure is well known. This not only places her before us against a background of esteem for herself, but in a reflection of the high regard and affection in which her father was held. Before matrimonial trials confronted her daughter, Mary Brewster, loved and loving, finished her pilgrimage; the lack of her presence affected many lives, her absence was an abiding sorrow. Love of wealth seems sud·denly to have overtaken Isaac Allerton which made everything else of small importance. The pursuit

of it took him constantly and for long periods away
from home, so his wife had little of his company.
His talents were of use to the colony, at times, in
England, but he seemed to really care very little
for his old friends. Nevertheless, it was he who
completed the arrangements which closed the connection between the original settlers of Plymouth
and the Merchant Adventurers in London. Plymouth, thereby, paid all its indebtedness for assistance
given and went its way alone. He also procured
patents for increased land holdings for the colony,
especially in Maine. His complete indifference to
anything but his own ends was, perhaps, never better
shown than when he returned from one of his trips
to England, bringing, as secretary, a man who was
already too well and unfavorably known by Plymouth and the surrounding settlements, called Morton of Merry Mount, who had been sent to England
the year before, as an undesirable. That Allerton
could bring this man to his home, into the society
of his wife and daughters, made Plymouth gasp —
and Plymouth refused to stand it. The secretary
was dismissed, and business affairs again called Isaac
Allerton away. On one of his trips he took his son
to visit in England, and Bartholomew did not return to Plymouth.

About this time, two girls of the *Anne* added to
the procession of brides: Mary Warren marrying
Robert Bartlett and Jane Cooke marrying Experience Mitchell.

Passengers and letters came on the ships continually, both to Plymouth and the other settlements that were growing likewise. Persons desiring to come to the New World, took what ship they could and landed where the ship took them. Plymouth having boats could always send for their own voyagers and mail whenever word was received that a ship had come from the other side, though not to their harbor. Thus, one day, a letter came to Humility Cooper, which changed the quiet current of her life as it seemed to be running in Plymouth. Relatives in England wanted her to return. This was a surprise to her and to her good friends, but, half wanting to stay and half wanting to go, Humility prepared for leave taking. Henry Sampson, her cousin, was now grown up — she need feel no special reluctance — but she was Elizabeth Howland's last link with her childhood's days. As Edward Winslow was sailing shortly for England, on business for the colony, Humility said farewell to the ten years of *Mayflower* and Plymouth association and went back under his care.

During her husband's absence, Susanna Winslow's brother, Doctor Fuller, was also from Plymouth. The new colonies of Salem and Massachusetts Bay, just starting, met with the same devastating illness that had befallen the *Mayflower* passengers, and, as they were so unfortunate as to lose their doctor among the first victims, they appealed to Plymouth—and no appeal to Plymouth was ever in vain. Doctor Fuller went to Salem and the Bay and had great success in curing many, though nearly exhausting his supply of medicines.

During this year, and the next, all the old friends still in Leyden, who had waited so long to come, were brought over at Plymouth's expense and there was great satisfaction that distance no longer divided them. But the saintly Robinson was not among them. Five years earlier, the Pilgrim men and women grieved to learn that he would never come to them — his earthly labors having ceased. His wife and oldest son became his representatives in Plymouth.

Intercourse between Plymouth and the newly established colonial neighbors became frequent, leading to interchange of visits and even of residence. The newcomers were duly sensible of what they owed to the Plymouth settlers, who had blazed the way.

The opening of their second decade in the New World showed great contrasts to those Plymouth women who remembered what the first year and those immediately following had been. Now, they were able to see and hear of the experiences of others, close at hand, with much in common. The ships from England were no longer their only connection with the outside world nor their only source of supplies, other than food. Massachusetts Bay and Salem were glad to exchange commodities, as well as Manhattan, but, being so much nearer, grew more interlocked with the life and interests of Plymouth.

The ceremonial visit by the Governor and Assistants of Plymouth to the Governor of the Bay and his wife, with the return of like courtesies by Governor Winthrop to Governor and Mrs. Bradford were brilliant incidents. Soon fashions, not clothes, and luxuries, not necessities, for the home were frequent thoughts to the women, instead of almost forgotten or sternly repressed instincts. Though they had not fashion books, some sent for garments and hats from the old country and the fortunate possessors lent these new fashioned articles as models for their neighbors. A very taking way of introducing styles to the colonists was by dressed dolls, or "babies" as they were called, that displayed them in careful miniature. During recent seasons this idea has been re-introduced, as may be seen in some of the shop windows in our cities. We learn that, withal, there was sometimes a shortage of sugar, which strikes a responsive chord in the memory of housewives three hundred years later.

If the arrival of the first cows was a never-to-be forgotten joy to the women of the *Mayflower* and of the *Anne,* the entrance of horses into Plymouth life was elation. The pleasure of owning a horse while it was a novelty for their circumstances, must have aroused the same feeling as the acquirement of an automobile has in families of our day; when not an owner, to have a special object of ambition, if a possessor, then a willing recipient of neighborly admiration. The advantage of a horse to a woman, then, was to ride on a pillion behind a male member of the family to meeting or to visit (until carriages came, much later), or else, if quite accomplished, to

ride alone, often with children, baskets, or even a
spinning wheel, as well, on the back of the amiable
friend of the family.

Ere long, life took on the virility and color we
associate with that spectacular period known as
Colonial. Naturally, Plymouth now began to over-
flow its first boundaries. As the children of the
families and worldly possessions increased, many
made summer homes where the cattle could have
greater range and families more room. These new
houses were built quite in the manner of bungalows,
for occupancy between frosts. Winters saw the
Plymouth residences occupied again. Gradually,
however, the summer homes became permanent, being made habitable for winter also, and edifices for
the religious services were erected. By another
decade Plymouth Colony comprised several towns,
outgrowths of the original. The new brides could
make a wedding journey if they pleased, and some
went away altogether to make their new homes. The
governor's wife was especially interested in two of
the weddings at this time — that of her sister, Priscilla Carpenter and her niece, Patience Morton.
The former was soon a widow, and, like her sisters,
married again. Patience became the mother of
Thomas Faunce — a link between two centuries —
the identifier, in his old age, of Plymouth Rock,
telling to his and other generations what his parents
had told to him, having learned from the first
comers.

Governor Bradford insisted that if the office he

had held so long was an honor and satisfaction, others should share it, if it was a care and duty, others should experience its responsibilities also; his health had been somewhat undermined by the efforts he had given to guide the temporal affairs of the colony throughout the years since he succeeded Governor Carver, and he absolutely declined a re-election. Edward Winslow, having returned from England, was chosen.

Thus Susanna became the first lady of Plymouth; easily pictured wearing the dainty white satin, lace trimmed slippers, or the white satin cape, actually to be seen now, in Plymouth, visible magic means of carrying us back to her days from the present. Alice Bradford smilingly relinquished her position to her friend and devoted her efforts to restoring her husband's health. Yet this twelve-month contained more of trial, anxiety and annoyance than the colony had experienced in many a year; it could not have been other than a sorrowful memory to Susanna.

Early in the spring a strange swarm of large noisy flies came out of the ground — ate the young green things, and disappeared. Such had never been seen by the colonists and the Indians foretold sickness. This prophecy proved all too true and during the summer and autumn a devastating fever swept away a score or more of men, women and children; some were of the new comers from Leyden, but the weight of the sadness was among the old families. Gentle Fear Brewster Allerton was laid

to rest beside her mother, on Burial Hill, leaving her
baby boy, Isaac, to her sorrowing father's care, who
was spending the summer with his two unmarried
sons on their farm in the country. Isaac Allerton's
sister, Sarah Cuthbertson, was also a victim to the
infection, likewise her husband. While Susanna
Winslow was mourning these two friends, her
brother, the doctor, after fighting the disease for the
help of others, succumbed. This shock and loss to
the colonists was felt not only in Plymouth — while
in Plymouth grief was deep. This educated,
Christian gentleman was sadly missed for many a
year. What he was to the people can be easily
imagined. His widow and children were devoted
to his memory; in after years, the son, Samuel,
studied for the ministry and married a granddaughter of Elder Brewster; the daughter, Mercy, married Ralph James; but his profession was carried
on in the Old Colony, after a time, by his nephews —
his namesake Samuel — whom we have known of
since the Pilgrims' emigration from Holland — and
Matthew, who came later to Plymouth.

The business affairs of the Colony became compli-
cated in their trade on the Connecticut River, both
because of the Dutch and Indians. At home, Roger
Williams, whom they had befriended, acted in a
very unpleasant manner, so they were glad when he
left them. Notwithstanding the clouds over-shadow-
ing them, this year's return of the trade in furs was
noteworthy, and as election time drew near, it was
decided that it would be best for Edward Winslow

to go again to England on their foreign business; therefore Thomas Prence was elected Governor and Susanna was again left alone with her children. The White boys were now sturdy, manly lads, a comfort and joy to Susanna and the admiration of their small brothers and sister, the Winslows. Another brother-in-law, Kenelm, was a visitor in her home, and appearances indicated that he would remain as a permanent resident of Plymouth.

Several marriages occurred before a year closed. Ann Warren became Mrs. Thomas Little and her sister, Sarah, became Mrs. John Cooke, Jr.

Recently a family of four girls had come to the colony with their father, William Collier, a wealthy merchant from London; from among them one of the Brewster boys selected his wife and Sarah Collier went as Love's bride to the Duxbury home to try to bring cheerfulness to the three lonely men there and to help care for little Isaac Allerton, his mother's legacy to her family, until he should grow up. Remember Allerton married also, and was one of the girls who went away from Plymouth to a new home in Salem, leaving her sister Mary, to give their father such attention as he needed in his rare visits home.

At this time, in Boston, eggs were three cents a dozen, milk one cent a quart, butter six and cheese five cents a pound, so housekeepers not caring for the somewhat higher prices in Plymouth, could send for butter or cheese at least, if they did not make it themselves, and felt economically inclined.

In the early part of the new administration, when
Patience Brewster Prence was mistress of the execu-
tive mansion (which was the Governor's own house,
whichever one it was), certain affairs concerned two
of the Plymouth women mightily, Priscilla Alden
and Barbara Standish, but particularly the former,
which was caused by the interference in Plymouth's
affairs by Massachusetts Bay, through misrepresen-
tation. John Alden putting into Boston from a trip
to the Kennebec trading station, was held there and
imprisoned until Plymouth should explain its connection with a shooting incident in which two men
were killed at the station. The ship was allowed to
return to Plymouth bringing the news of this cool
proceeding, which, we can imagine made John Alden's wife anything but cool, and we can also think
that the Governor was not allowed to delay in getting John Alden home to his family. To do so,
Captain Myles Standish was dispatched to Boston,
with the facts of the unpleasant incident at the
trading station, which were so different from the
representation which the Bay authorities had received that John Alden was immediately set at
liberty. We can appreciate the feelings of both
Barbara and Priscilla as they looked for the return
of the ship again. Barbara anxious for the success
of her husband's efforts to release the husband of
her friend, and Priscilla both indignant and wor-
ried. However, the incident was happily concluded,
though more than Priscilla were indignant in Plymouth.

Later in the year, news came from London which caused the heart of Susanna to burn with indignation in her turn, and for the same cause concerning her husband as had agitated Priscilla. Through the old jealousy of the Church authorities, on trumped up charges concerning the business on which Winslow went to England, which was in behalf also of the Bay, he was held for many weeks in the Fleet Street prison. Fortunately friends were able to release him — but it was some time before he was able to return to his family in Plymouth.

Meanwhile Eleanor Newton Adams and Priscilla Carpenter Wright, both made widows by the epidemic of the previous year, became wives again. The marriage of the former, who had been left quite well off, was of special interest to Susanna since she became her sister-in-law, Mrs. Kenelm Winslow, the third Mrs. Winslow of Plymouth and Marshfield, as all had summer places in the latter suburb of Plymouth——Careswell, the Edward Winslow place, soon became a permanent abode, handsome of style and proportions.

This year saw sorrow once more fall on the members of the old families — bound together by the powerful ties formed in the old days — and many more, for at its close, the Governor's wife was taken by death — and Patience Brewster Prence's short, happy life was over. The religious convictions of the Pilgrims did not admit of undue mourning for their loved ones, since they regarded the departed not as victims to death, but as victors through death,

and the lives of those remaining must go on. Hearts
were true, nevertheless, and even in their wills the
men sometimes especially requested to be laid beside
the graves of their wives and daughters.

The following year, April, brought a marriage
ceremony performed by Captain Standish, as assistant, which was of interest to many — that of
Samuel Fuller, loved for his own admirable qualities
as well as for being the nephew of their Doctor of
happy memory. His bride was one of the girls who
had helped in the new settlement of Scituate, found-
ed by her father and other men from Kent, in England. In spite of all his pretty playmates in Plymouth, Samuel found this girl of old England was
the one to receive his heart. But Jane Lothrop took
him from Plymouth to the newer township.

In August a furious storm broke over Plymouth
and the surrounding land and sea, inflicting great
damage and terrifying the women and children. It
wrecked many ships, killed cattle and blew roofs
from many of the houses and knocked others to
pieces in Plymouth, and uprooted quantities of great
trees; the evidences of it were prominent for many
years in the blemished beauty of the great pines
which withstood the hurricane, still remaining the
sentinels of Plymouth.

When Edward Winslow returned, he again served
as Governor, and one of the weddings of that year
was Mary Allerton's. She was last but one of the
Mayflower girls to marry — Damaris Hopkins'
marriage to Jacob Cooke completed the list. Mary's

courtship had begun in childhood's days, when
Thomas Cushman, in the house across the street, had
waited for her to grow up — while growing up himself and pursuing his studies with the other boys in
the Governor's family. At the time of her marriage
the rumblings of the Pequot war were beginning to
be heard, which soon broke, owing to the mistakes of
the Bay Colony, causing the old time fears to return
to Plymouth women for the safety of their men and
themselves. Under Captain Standish, the Plymouth
men played their valiant part, and Thomas Stanton,
the interpreter for Massachusetts, and Captain John
Gallup did their full share to redeem the situation.

Richard Church had not long before come from
the Bay Colony to visit Plymouth, but meeting
Elizabeth Warren decided him to remain permanently, in spite of displeasure from the Bay authorities, who missed him. He was one of the
Plymouth fighters in this Indian disturbance, as his
and Elizabeth's son, Benjamin, was in the greater,
bloodier war of a later time — King Philip's — when
the Pilgrim's good friend, Massasoit, was dead.
Plymouth tried to settle down to its own affairs after
this, and had plenty to attend to.

A lovely June day seemed ushering in another
summer when an unknown experience marked that
year as one to date by even as the one of the great
storm. That morning some of the principal men
were meeting to discuss important questions, and in
the street and about the doorsteps many of the
women were talking of their own or public affairs,

when a violent though brief earthquake shook them
from their balance, and catching hold of whatever
was nearest, they heard the crashing and falling of
things in their houses. The children were frightened and began to cry, and all the women who were
indoors came running out, fearing the houses would
fall.   The men were no less concerned and the
streets presented a lively scene. Another shock was
soon felt but less severe, and that was the end.
Indians came hurrying into the town with their experience to relate; the quake was felt far inland
and at sea. What with the frightful storm, the
alarming Pequot trouble and this terrifying experience, all within a comparatively short time, the
nerves of the women must have been more on edge
than for many a day.

The young people of Marshfield and Duxbury,
married and single, clung closely to their friends
and associations of Plymouth and their amusements
were shared in common. Weekly lecture day, a
diversion of sober character, was nevertheless gladly
welcomed as a means of enjoyable intercourse, going
or returning. Maple sugar making, Training day,
corn husking, apple bees were occasions for merry
gatherings, the sequence found in the frequent weddings. Dancing became popular, though frowned on
in some quarters, but it could not be repressed in
an age when the desire for physical activity and excitement was as natural as now. Some of those
early dance names such as High Betty Martin, Con-
stancy, Orange Tree, Rolling Hornpipe, The Ladies

Choice, compare with our recent names of Hesita-
tion, Fox Trot, One Step.

The Coast Road from Boston, though never more
than a few feet wider than the old Indian trail,
came to mean to the dwellers in the various town-
ships of Plymouth such an artery of connection to
the life of all as the Great North Road had been to
the inhabitants of the little villages, Scrooby and its
neighbors, long ago homes to the elder members of
the Colony.

The coldest winter Plymouth has ever known has
frozen the harbor to a solid mass over which ox
teams and sledges have been driven for several
weeks, an astonishing and interesting sight and one
may walk over the ice to Duxbury as well as by the
land. One afternoon bright with the lengthening
daylight of the season, sees a pleasant picture in the
old parlor of Governor Bradford's house, for he is
again Governor, by urgent request of the community. A cheery fire blazes up the wide chimney and
there is gay chatter to the tune of the crackling logs.
Mistress Alice Bradford, now a grandmother (her
son, Constant Southworth having married Elizabeth
Collier and having a little Alice) has invited several
of her daughter's special friends to spend the day.
So we see Mercy, a delightful reproduction of her
mother and father both, as hostess to nine merry
girls: Mary Brewster, Betty and Sally Alden, from
Duxbury, Mary Cooke, Mercy Fuller and Deborah
Hopkins of Plymouth, Lora Standish of Duxbury

and Desire and Hope Howland. Elizabeth Tilly
had given charming companion names to her older
daughters, her first born having been named in
remembrance of Desire Minter, her dear friend.
Desire was now at the age of her mother when she
had married — that mother seeming always as an
older sister, being still young herself in spite of the
cares of a large family — but it was more than a
year later before Desire decided to marry, and be
the first bride, though not the eldest, of this pretty
group. The girls of this generation never having
experienced the world's hardships and vicissitudes
that had been their mother's portions, having been
carefully and lovingly brought up in comfortable,
cheerful homes, were not anxious to leave them for
the first time, even with love to point the way.
However, Desire was beginning to listen to the im-
portunities of her dashing young lieutenant — in
later years known as Captain John Gorham, who
was to lead the 2nd Barnstable Company under
command of Major William Bradford, Mercy's
brother, into fame, at the Great Swamp Fight in
Philip's War. The swift knitting needles click in
Desire's hands as she stands by the frame-work of
the western window, leaning to watch the progress
of the sampler which is being worked by a lovely
girl who is sharing the broad window seat with
another, who has evidently completed her sewing,
having just folded it and put it into a bag hanging
from her arm. This young beauty is Betty Alden —
eldest of the family of John and Priscilla. She too,

is eagerly watching the stitches that are to tell the worker's admirers and friends, from that day to this, that the sampler was made by Lora Standish, only and much beloved daughter of the Pilgrim's Captain. That piece of handicraft is the only specimen of their work that we know of and may look at today as if we had seen it when its stitches were being placed, among the group we are picturing of Plymouth Colony's first-born daughters — the first native generation of Colonial girls of New England. On a seat by the hearth, Mary Cooke and Mercy Fuller have a book between them and are reading aloud snatches of receipts for making perfumes, or poetry, or jokes — this is not a monthly magazine as we might fancy from our own experience, but a yearly periodical, welcomed by every household — Pierce's Almanac, printed in Cambridge, its contents holding much that is similar but much that is different to the magazines we know. Leaning over the high back, smoothing the soft hair of Mercy Fuller, is Hope Howland. Bonny as her sister is, somehow Hope reminds us more of little Elizabeth Tilly of Leyden. Mercy Bradford is placing little cakes with a pitcher of cider on a big center table and lights one or two bayberry candles in wooden holders that stand upon its polished top and twinkle on it or in the shining pewter dishes and cups. At the window towards the street, Deborah Hopkins and Mary Brewster, granddaughter and namesake of our first Mary Brewster, are looking out — evidently some one is expected. The last rays of the winter sun, the flashing fire and the glowing bayberry flames, strive to light for one more instant this appealing picture. There is sound of footsteps in the cold air outside — stamping and laughing — the brothers and sweethearts have arrived to take the girls home but first to have some slight refreshment at the hands of Mistress Bradford and Mercy. Cloaks are brought and velvet hoods tied snugly over hair both light and dark, surrounding the pink cheeks and sparkling eyes of all the happy girls who have spent the day with Mercy Bradford and her mother.

The snowflakes of winter have turned to falling apple blossoms and spring has awakened the violets in the flower beds under the windows of William Brewster's library. The fragrance of these and other blossoms is borne through the white curtained windows open to the warm air, mingled with the saltness of Duxbury marshes. The library comprises four hundred books, the largest and most valuable in America. Whether it is or no, matters not, the books are the solace of their owner, who while enjoying his farm life and appreciating the companionship of his son's families and Isaac Allerton, Jr., his grandson, dwells much within himself. To keep the books dusted and the Elder's chair in just the right place, Mrs. Love Brewster has often the assistance of her nieces, Jonathan Brewster's daughters. This bright morning sees Mary, one of the girls in the winter's frolic at Mercy Bradford's, attending to these matters. A boy is deep in study by a bookshelf, and Mary, playfully sweeps her duster across his book as she works — it is her cousin, Isaac — preparing for entrance into the new College at Cambridge. Up the road a horse comes at a lively pace and Samuel Fuller has arrived to join with Isaac in reading the precious books, though his father left him some of his own. The owner of the library glances through the window and smiles and nods to the young people — Mary seeing him, runs out to enjoy with him the sunshine and to pat the horse tied near the door. Possibly William Brewster recalls from the past a spring morning when another lad rode a horse, to acquire knowledge from books — but he says nothing as Mary slips her arm in his.

This decade flashes many another change before our eyes. In a few years the first church building has been erected in Plymouth, with Richard Church as architect and builder, as seems appropriate. Its bell rings out for many a year, succeeding the roll of drums to summon worshipers. Many of the girls marry and the younger children succeed to their pleasures. Mercy Bradford has gone to live in Boston as Mercy Vermayes. Her mother's loneliness is partly relieved by the coming to her of her remaining sister in England, Mary Carpenter. This sister is rather notable among the women of Plymouth, in that she never married. Her attractions were not less than her sisters'; indeed, from what was said of her, quite an appropriate companion for the governor's wife, her sister, Alice. Another exception to

the general rule may be noted, and another spinster
of the colony named Elizabeth Pool, daughter of Sir
William, who coming as Plymouth's boundaries ex-
panded, and possessing wealth, property and intelligence, remained unwon. These two esteemed women, one a resident of Plymouth town, the other,
one of the founders of the new township of Taunton, are an interesting contrast. Miss Carpenter
lived quietly, uneventfully, until ninety years old;
of a religious frame of mind and given to kind deeds,
unknown, through her retiring nature. Miss Pool
seems much more modern in her career. She erected
iron works and was altogether enterprising and a
promoter of advancement for her settlement. She
brought over a minister for the church in Taunton,
so had a thought for religion, also, not only for herself but for others. A record states "she died
greatly honored, in 1654 aged 66."

Edward Winslow was again governor for a brief
period and then made another trip to England, at
the request of the authorities of the Bay, as they
had recognized his great abilities as a negotiator of
business interests and there were some affairs press-
ing on the Bay Colony which he undertook to
remove. This was to the regret of the Plymouth
people who were reluctant to have him go from
their own affairs. He left Susanna and his children,
almost grown now, in comfortable Careswell, and
there, for several years, his wife awaited his return.
Not that the Bay or his own affairs took very long,
but England herself needed him, as it seemed, and

he agreed to a diplomatic mission to an island colony. Loving Plymouth and loving England he was not destined to rest in either; his grave was made in the ocean he had crossed so often. Susanna had parted from her husband for the last time.

Other deaths among the first comers saddened the Pilgrims. Elizabeth Hopkins closed her long and honorable career as one of the women of Plymouth. Her husband soon followed her. In this year perhaps its greatest blow fell on Plymouth when their leader in spiritual and often advisor in temporal things passed from among them. No words can more fittingly describe the beautiful end of his earthly life than those of the governor. There is no greater record of loyalty and affection than that shown in the nearly fifty years between his followers and himself. While his fame, as William Bradford said, is more enduring than a marker at his grave — which he lacks, in company with so many — such words as the governor wrote of him and such work as Constantino Brumidi has made to represent him, serve to keep it vigorous through the centuries. (In the President's room at the Capitol in Washington, Brumidi has painted Elder Brewster as typifying Religion.)

When Mary Chilton Winslow moved to Boston, it could not have seemed more strange or different than Plymouth had come to be to her by that time. Except the Aldens, the Howlands and her sister-in-law, few remained who had been her companions and friends on the *Mayflower* and in building the

colony. Her husband had become a prosperous merchant in the West India trade and perhaps Boston
seemed a necessary relief to them. Their position
became at once prominent and important and her
life flowed happily onward for many years. In one
of her daughters, Myles Standish, Jr., found his fate,
and upon their marriage likewise settled in Boston.

Meanwhile Susanna Winslow continued in eminence of circumstance, to live at her beautiful home
in Marshfield. Her boys, Resolved and Peregrine,
had married and made homes of their own but remained devoted to her. Josiah, her youngest son,
reproducing in a marked degree the look and manners of his talented father, remained with her. As
he grew into the handsome, courtly man, whom all
admired, she must have smiled as she looked sometimes at the little shoes he had worn as her baby and
which she carefully kept with other treasures —
such as the cradle in which she had rocked all her
boys and little girl. That little girl was now Mrs.
Robert Brooks of Scituate.

In the heyday of Plymouth's prosperity a gentleman in England, long interested in colonial life by
the reports of it which had found their way to him
in his comfortable ancestral home, planned a visit
to see life across the sea. With his young daughter,
Penelope, Mr. Herbert Pelham came to the Old
Colony. The spirit of adventure in them both and
the interest they found in their new surroundings
caused them to linger for a period beyond the length
of a casual visit in their temporary home in Marsh-

field. To the men, the companionship of Herbert
Pelham was a delight, and seeing her father's pleasure, Penelope, with her own various employments,
did not long for home. Her's is the last romance
we may notice as closely connected with the women
of our special interest in Plymouth colony, even
as that of her mother-in-law, was the first. Penelope Pelham, with her high-bred manner and aristocratic face, made the only permanent impression on
the heart of Josiah Winslow and we can easily fancy
that in making her bead bag, Penelope had plenty
of time to decide that for him she would renounce
all thought of returning to her home, and remain a
colonial woman. The bead bag, her dressing-case
and her portrait are other links connecting us to
those vivid lives of our chronicle.

Soon Josiah Winslow was called to the place occupied by his father, for a time, and by William Bradford for many years — when the great governor had
left it vacant, forever — so Penelope became the
first lady of the land in her adopted home and
Susanna closed her life's history in the first place
which had been hers so often in the colony — first
mother after the *Mayflower* found harbor, first bride
of Plymouth and now mother of the first native
born governor of New England. Truly the foot-
prints of Anna Fuller, since we found them first
in Leyden, have led us along a colorful pathway.

The records we find of her brilliant daughter-in-
law show her a character after Susanna Winslow's
own type. The second mistress of Careswell lived

there for many happy years ere she and her family were forced to flee from it under the fearful scourge of Philip's War.

Thus on through its seventy years of shadow and sunshine, heroic daring, splendid achievement and independence, we may follow the fascinating records of Plymouth Colony — especially as those records are tinted even faintly by the foot-prints and finger-touches of its women.

As the first death on the *Mayflower* at anchor was that of a woman, Dorothy Bradford, so the last survivor of the original *Mayflower* company was a woman, Mary Allerton Cushman, who saw all of the life with its chances and changes of which we read.

Through the years we may well believe that the women of the *Mayflower* who became the women of Plymouth, and their children, whether in newer homes or remaining in the old, looked back to the early days of their privation, when by their anxieties, their sorrows, their economies, their endeavors, their fearlessness and faith, the foundation of their colony was laid.

We may well echo their thoughts as they remembered some of Elder Brewster's words on their first Thanksgiving Day, which one orator has expressed as "Generations to come will look back to this hour and these scenes, this day of small things and say, 'Here was our beginning as a people. These were our fathers and mothers. Through their trials we inherit our blessings. Their faith is our faith, their hope our hope, their God our God.' "

A CHAPLET OF ROSEMARY.

A CHAPLET OF ROSEMARY.

BURIAL HILL no longer bristles with the guns of the Pilgrim's fort but is thickly studded with the graves of the generations who in turn walked on Plymouth's first street below. One traversing this way and recalling the scenes it has witnessed, must be indeed insensitive not to feel the thrill that comes from treading on hallowed ground. Particularly must this be experienced by the descendants of the women we would honor.

We know that upon Cole's Hill, Burial Hill and in the old burying grounds at Duxbury and Marshfield are the graves of many of the women of Plymouth, and some lie elsewhere, yet the exact location of how few is positive.

The second wife of Governor Bradford requested in her will that she might be laid as near her husband's grave as might be. Their family plot is easily found. By another will, that of Captain Myles Standish, we may know where two of the women of his family rest — since his own grave is located and his request was to lie beside his two dear daughters — one his son's wife Mary, the other his own lovely Lora, whose early death caused him much sorrow. At Marshfield, in the family burying ground, Susanna Winslow rests. A stone in the center of the town of Taunton marks the grave of Elizabeth Pool. A tablet at Little Compton, has been erected to the memory of Elizabeth Pabodie, John and Priscilla Alden's eldest daughter; she lived her later years in this place. Mary Chilton Winslow lies beside her husband, in King's Chapel Burying Ground, Boston; their names are marked upon a slab at the gate in Tremont Street. Elizabeth Tilly Howland, after she became a widow, went to live with her daughter, Lydia Brown, in Swansea and there died; her husband's grave on Burial Hill is known, but she was not brought back to rest beside him. The grave of Mary Allerton, who lived to such a great age and saw the foundations of twelve of the thirteen colonies which formed the nucleus of the United States, is indicated by a monument erected to her and her husband on Burial Hill.

We would willingly make a pilgrimage to visit each known spot, regretting, the while, that there were so many we might not include. Yet upon all we may place the same unfading, if invisible, wreath of the leaves that signify remembrance.

Descendants of the women of Plymouth are now estimated to number more than a million. It is for them especially to rejoice in the results of artist's brush, writer's pen or sculptor's tool that have been produced in efforts to recall to all the world that epoch in its history in which these women lived, by portraying the events of which they were a part.

Thus we have such pictures as Jacob and Albert Cuyp's painting of the "Departure of the Pilgrims from Delfshaven." J. G. Schwartz's picture of

"The Pilgrim Fathers' First Meeting for Public Worship in North America." "The Embarkation of the Pilgrim Fathers," painted by Charles W. Cope, hangs in the British House of Parliament. "The Sailing of the Mayflower," a painting in the audit house, Southampton, England — no more appropriate setting could be found for that portrayal. Charles Lucy has called his picture "Departure of the Pilgrims," it is in Pilgrim Hall, Plymouth — that Memorial temple. Robert W. Wier's painting of "Embarkation of the Pilgrims" hangs in the nation's Capitol, while Edgar Parker's copy of it is in Pilgrim Hall. A. Gisbert has given us his idea of the "Landing of the Pilgrim Fathers at Plymouth Rock," and the "Landing of the Pilgrim Fathers" is the title taken by Henry Sargent. "The Mayflower in Plymouth Harbor," is portrayed by W. F. Halsall, and Granville Perkins has visualized "The Mayflower at Sea," while Linton has engraved this subject. George H. Boughton has made charming and familiar reproductions of the Pilgrim men and women, and many another artist's ideal has been depicted in the variations of the subject.

Fiction, verse and chronicle with the themes of the voyage and the Plymouth home of the Pilgrims have been produced by many able pens. Skillful historians, essayists, orators have done justice to the men; the events entering into their lives, the courage and valor which each day brought forth, have been recorded with emphasis and unflagging zeal. We are indeed glad and appreciative of the constant narration of the facts with which we have become familiar. At the same time, the regret comes to us that of the women so little has been said; that the balance of the two groups of the colony builders has not been better kept.

Of the Fathers we are accustomed to hear, but our gratitude salutes those who occasionally mention the Mothers and Daughters. They were two characteristic notes in the making of that Pilgrim score but because the latter was more lightly struck it has been too lightly regarded. Nevertheless, we rejoice that we know as much as we do of the women, and in the knowledge that increasing recognition is being given them.

Recently a plan was made that a chime of bells should be placed in the tower of the Pilgrim Monument at Provincetown and dedicated to the Women of the *Mayflower* by their descendants. More recently still, Henry H. Kitson has modeled a statue of a Pilgrim Woman for erection at Plymouth, in their memory. We may recall here the noble monument erected by the nation to the Pilgrims. In this design a woman is the exalted figure who holds the book and gazes over the sea. Also of the four important though lesser figures, two are women. Hon. John D. Long has said of the heroic figure, "Her eyes look toward the sea. Forever she beholds upon its waves the incoming *"Mayflower,"* she sees the Pilgrims land. They vanish, but she, the monument of their faith remains and tells their story to the world," which, as another has said, "in romance of

circumstance and charm of personal heroism . . .
is pre-eminent.''

Well may be seen the qualities of heart and mind
reproduced in countless of their descendants who
have carried on the influence of their personality
and work, deepening its roots down through the
years. ''The light they kindled has shone to many,
in some degree to our whole nation.'' In proof of
this is a relation of some who have claimed descent
from a Pilgrim of the *Mayflower* or of Plymouth.
This will comprise Presidents of the United States,
presidents of universities or colleges, jurists, dip-
lomats, writers, artists, military and naval men of
all our wars, governors of states, church dignita·
ries, physicians, scientists, senators, representatives,
signers of the Declaration of Independence, makers
of the Constitution. It is difficult to begin, more so
to pause, in such a list.

Annie A. Haxtun has said of one to be mentioned,
''John Tilly's spirit of adventure has fallen upon
one, at least of his descendants, General A. W.
Greely, the Arctic explorer, watched over by the
God of his Pilgrim forefathers, was saved by the
naval relief expedition to do good to the country,
which is his on a claim of more than two centuries.''
It is John and Hope Chipman, daughter of John
and Elizabeth Tilly Howland, who are also ancestors of General Greely; and it may here be said that
it is partly through his suggestion that the subject
of this work was projected (in the smaller form of
its first appearance) ; the other descendant likewise

responsible was Mr. William Lowrie Marsh, of Washington, D. C., founder of the Society of Mayflower Descendants in that city; the ancestors of Mr. Marsh were William and Alice Bradford.

John and Priscilla Alden, William and Mary Brewster, Richard and Elizabeth Warren and Francis and Hester Cooke have as their descendants those who have been Presidents of the Republic: John Adams and John Quincy Adams, Zachary Taylor, Ulysses Simpson Grant and William Howard Taft. Also from the Aldens have descended President Wheelock of Dartmouth College and President Kirkland of Harvard.

Bishop Soule of the Methodist Church is in line of descent from George Soule and his wife.

Descendants of Giles Hopkins and Catherine Wheeldon have added distinction to the family. Stephen Hopkins, great grandson of the original, again made the name famous by placing it among the signers of the Declaration of Independence, while his brother, Ezekiel, became the first admiral of our national navy. At the present time it is important through Colonel Thomas S. Hopkins, a veteran of the Civil War, past Governor-General of the General Society of Mayflower Descendants and a prominent lawyer and resident of Washington, D. C.

In Washington, also, Mr. Ernest W. Bradford, an able patent lawyer, continues the eminence of the name of his ancestors. Washington, likewise, is the residence of Mr. A. A. Aspinwall, historian of that city's Society of Mayflower Descendants, representing John and Elizabeth Howland.

A descendant of Francis and Hester Cooke is Major General Leonard Wood, at present Governor-General of the General Society of Mayflower Descendants.

The late Hon. Levi P. Morton, one time governor of New York State and Vice-President of the United States, was descended from the Hopkins and Cooke as well as Morton families.

From John and Priscilla Alden have come the poets William Cullen Bryant and Henry Wadsworth Longfellow, and the first Bishop of the Episcopal Church in America, Samuel Seabury; also the Revolutionary War Generals, Joseph and James Warren, the former of Bunker Hill fame, the latter President of the Congress of Massachusetts and husband of Mercy Otis, writer and patriot. Benjamin Church on whom the mantle of Myles Standish fell as Plymouth's military leader, was the son of Elizabeth Warren and Richard Church.

In line of descent from Mary and William Brewster is a family of North Carolina, interesting in three generations, Chief Justice Richmond Mumford Pearson, Hon. Richmond Pearson, Envoy Extraordinary and Minister Plenipotentiary of the United States to Persia, Captain Richmond Pearson Hobson, a hero of the Spanish American War.

From them also is Donald Grant Mitchel, author, Lieut. Alden Davidson, an aviator in the World War died for his country; as his name implies, John and

Priscilla Alden were his ancestors. A great great granddaughter of theirs was Faith Robinson; she married Governor Trumbull of Connecticut, George Washington's "Brother Jonathan" which name gradually became a synonym for a typical American. She gained fame for giving her scarlet cloak at a church collection for the army, in which she was decidedly interested, having three sons as officers. Her fourth son was the famous artist. Mrs. May Alden Ward, author, was a descendant in a recent generation.

From Mary (Allerton) and Thomas Cushman came America's famous tragedienne, Charlotte Cushman; also Mr. Cushman K. Davis, Governor of Minnesota, who made the speech of dedication at the ceremonies connected with the Cushman Monument on Burial Hill.

From Constance Hopkins and her husband Nicholas Snow, Robert Treat Paine, signer of the Declaration of Independance, and Robert Treat Paine, poet were descended.

In the convention which framed the Constitution John Tilly and the Howlands were represented by their descendant — through Desire Howland and Captain John Gorham — Nathaniel Gorham, who, as a member, was several times requested by General Washington to occupy the chair.

From this same group came Bishop Philips Brooks. As it is said, John Howland came to this country in the capacity of secretary to Governor John Carver, one, at least, of his and Elizabeth's

descendants filled that position toward another ce-
lebrity. Edward Herbert Noyes, journalist and
traveller, first returned to the land of his ancestors
as private secretary to Hon. John Lothrop Motley,
historian and diplomatist, United States Ambassador to the Court of St. James. Rev. Thomas
Clap, fourth President of Yale College, was also
of the line of Howland, while his wife, Mary
Whiting, was descended from Governor Bradford
and his wife.

From Mary Chilton and her husband John Wins-
low, comes Mrs. Robert Hall Wiles, of Chicago, past
President of the National Society of United States
Daughters of the War of 1812 and now serving as
President-General of the National Society Daugh-
ters of Founders and Patriots of America. From
Mary and John Winslow, also, came Lieutenant
Sturdevant, another young aviator of the World
War, killed over-seas in the service of his country.

For another repetion of the exact name of his an
cestor there is Doctor Myles Standish, a noted
occulist of Boston. In the medical profession also
Doctor Stuart Clark Johnson of Washington and
Doctor Ira Hart Noyes of Providence, the first from
John and Priscilla Alden, the second from John and
Elizabeth Howland, both answering the call of duty
to country in the World War, to serve over-seas.

Two residents of Washington are Hon. William S.
Washburne — United States Civil Service Commis-
sioner and Mr. Frank Herbert Briggs of the Court
of Claims — descended respectively from Francis

and Hester Cooke, and the Brewster, Bradford and Alden families.

The late Henry Billings Brown, Associate Justice of the Supreme Court of the United States was another descendant of John and Elizabeth Howland while the late Seth Shepherd, Chief Justice of the Court of Appeals of the District of Columbia, was another representative of the line of William and Mary Brewster. Mr. A. Howard Clark, who was editor of the magazine of the Smithsonian Institution, was a descendant from the Brewsters, Hopkins and Howlands. The name of Howland Davis tells plainly why he has done so much for present day Plymouth and the Society of Mayflower Descendants.

In the United States Senate are three prominent descendants of the Pilgrims. The ancestors of Senator Henry Cabot Lodge of Massachusetts, chairman of Committee on Foreign Relations, are John and Elizabeth Tilly Howland. The Senators from New York and Vermont, Hon. James Wolcott Wadsworth, Jr., and Hon. Carroll Smally Page, are descendants respectively from Giles and Catharine Hopkins and William and Mary Brewster.

A descendant in the person of William Wallace Case, has visited Scrooby and brought from there a piece of oak once a part of the old Manor house, home of his ancestors, William and Mary Brewster — this priceless relic has been made into the gavel used by the Governor of the District of Columbia Society of Mayflower Descendants.

In hundreds of cities and towns and villages of the nation there are other and equally consistent representatives of the glorious names of their Plymouth ancestors. As we have seen the men in all the branches of service to their country, the women may be compared no less favorably in what they have rendered. In their nation's wars, they have ever been faithful, and their efforts as beneficial to the men and cause as were those of their ancestors of their own sex, whose work was as the mortar in the solid foundation wall of the nation they helped to build. Someone has said that always in the history of mankind the woman has been at her best when she has felt herself most needed. Every reason then for her to attract as she appears in pioneer days, in those of the Revolution or War for the Union and in the World War, unfailingly illustrating, unconsciously or not, the age old motto of *Noblesse Oblige*.

In hamlet or city, women descendants of Plymouth women upheld the honor of their men and country in Red Cross, Government Loans or ''Y.'' work during the World War. In the Sanitary Commission and Nursing Units of the Civil War the women's spirit was the same, and in 1776 when their days were nearest to the pioneer women, the women of the Revolutionary War inheriting the courage and self-forgetfulness, matched the heroism of the men. Thus each generation of women has met the crisis actuated by the same unanimity of purpose and devotion — from each in turn their successors have caught the falling torch, assuring that they shall not have lived and worked in vain. And they may sleep in peace.

The American women of today must meet the challenge of the women of 1861, 1776 and 1620. She must bear comparison with them in fundamental things. Patriotism, firmness, thrift, decision and re-sourcefulness, characteristics which are their heritage. As someone has said, "We are living in the tomorrow for which they wrought. We are to do today with all fidelity each bit of work which lies at our hands. This will make our next day brighter and by so much, set the world forward."

The mission of the *Mayflower* company was to open the way for a successful colonization of the New World. Its mission was faithfully performed. In studying the details and circumstances relating to the immortal voyage and settlement of Plymouth — particularly in relation to the women, vested to-day with supreme interest and in a glamour peculiarly their own, we must feel that that nobility of life may be ours as well as theirs and that it may illuminate the difficult life of today and make it worthy to be the fruit of the tree of Liberty they helped to plant, in tears and smiles.

Realizing the heavy debt that we owe to the men who were led to undertake the settlement of Plymouth we owe an equal if not greater debt to the women who had the courage and spirit to enter with them into the great and epoch making adventure. These make the shrines which we would visit. It is with reverence that we view not only the soil which first they trod but every spot associated with them.

If history as some one has said is in its unchangeable essence a tale, then this particular history is a tale that cannot be too often told or heard, not merely to hold our attention to the past but by its light to look forward with a thrill to the future, to the tasks and service for civilization, under the Providence by which the women of the *Mayflower* and the women of Plymouth were upheld. This will be the best memorial we can give these women all through the years; the remembrance that cannot fade.

CPSIA information can be obtained
at www.ICGtesting.com
Printed in the USA
BVHW032224260820
587434BV00002B/613

9 789353 703615